WildLife

Also by Pat Neal

WildLife Volume 1

The Fisherman's Prayer

WildLife Volume 2 The Mountain Pond.

WildLife

Volume 3: The Fisherman's Holidays

PAT NEAL

WILDLIFE
VOLUME 3: THE FISHERMAN'S HOLIDAYS

iUniverse books may be ordered through booksellers or by contacting:

iUniverse
1663 Liberty Drive
Bloomington, IN 47403
www.iuniverse.com
1-800-Authors (1-800-288-4677)

Because of the dynamic nature of the Internet, any web addresses or links contained in this book may have changed since publication and may no longer be valid. The views expressed in this work are solely those of the author and do not necessarily reflect the views of the publisher, and the publisher hereby disclaims any responsibility for them.

Any people depicted in stock imagery provided by Thinkstock are models, and such images are being used for illustrative purposes only. Certain stock imagery © Thinkstock.

ISBN: 978-1-5320-3316-2 (sc)
ISBN: 978-1-5320-3318-6 (hc)
ISBN: 978-1-5320-3317-9 (e)

Library of Congress Control Number: 2017914393

Print information available on the last page.

iUniverse rev. date: 10/03/2017

DEDICATION

For Steve and Sally.

INTRODUCTION

Thank you for reading this. Momma always said if you can't say something nice write for the newspaper, so I did. Writing a weekly wilderness gossip column was fun for a week or so. Then I ran out of stuff you could put in a newspaper. I started writing about holidays, fisherman's holidays. Fishermen like holidays because they keep other folks off the water. The way we celebrate traditional holidays like Thanksgiving, obscure holidays like Arbor Day and as yet to be declared holidays like National Cabin Fever Day depends on whether you fish or not. The first day of school was not a holiday for me but I'll bet it was for my mother. Written from my research as an historian and the wild and wooly life of a guide on the rivers of the Olympic Peninsula, these stories attempt to answer the eternal question: why can't the Skunk Cabbage Festival last all year? Gleaned from the commentary page of The Peninsula Daily News, here's a year's worth of Fisherman's Holiday stories. I hope you like them.

TABLE OF CONTENTS

ILLUSTRATIONS

NATIONAL CABIN FEVER DAY.

It's official. The cabin fever season started early this year, attacking the Olympic Peninsula in a vice-like grip that shows no sign of weakening in the foreseeable future. Cabin Fever Syndrome is a common, chronic, poly-phobic seasonal disorder that can make its appearance about the time the last Christmas cookie crumbles. Experts agree that the early appearance of this disorder might have been caused by the toughest winter in twenty-five years. The severity of this hard winter was predicted in my wilderness gossip column last autumn based on the number and size of spiders and the thick layers of fat on deer and mountain trout. That's how I knew my own cabin fever was coming on: I was writing a newspaper column about writing a newspaper column. Which spawned a movement to declare a National Cabin Fever Day to spotlight the insidious danger of this disease.

The latest research on this curious condition confirms a coincidence of congenital characteristics contravening conventional clinical concerns of a catatonic convalescence. There are many theories on the origin of CFS. Whether it's the sudden change from a diet consisting solely of Christmas fudge or light deprivation associated with the final unplugging of the Christmas lights, CFS can reduce an otherwise healthy individual to a zombie-like couch tuber whose motor skills have dwindled to twitching the remote control and opening another tub of ice cream. CFS victims often appear confused and bloated because they are. These patients can exhibit a wide range of symptoms that include drowsiness, insomnia and a brain numbness. CFS victims are often unaware they have a problem until they begin hoarding hot water bottles, darning their socks and watching old movies.

The more advanced cases of CFS are often convinced that winter will never end. Knowing you have CFS is the first step in finding a cure. It's not something you have to be ashamed of anymore. For too long cabin fever sufferers have been unfairly labeled lazy no-good-for-nothings who can't get out of bed in the morning and pull ourselves up by our own bootstraps because we can't find our boots.

Many so-called experts will tell you they have a cure for cabin fever and I must have tried them all. I consumed massive amounts of fudge. That was supposed to fool the brain into thinking it was still consuming Christmas fudge by short-circuiting the toggle switch mechanism inside the brain muscle itself. I vacationed in a tropical paradise which would have cured the cabin fever if I hadn't made the mistake of coming back to the cold and gray of our endless winter. I thought all these so-called cures for cabin fever were nothing but self-defeating wastes of time.

Then I received an invitation to go razor clam digging at night, in the middle of winter on a remote beach along the storm-tossed Pacific Ocean. I thought they were nuts but no, they were clam diggers. Maybe it's just because they are too busy trying to keep warm, but razor clam diggers never seem to suffer from Cabin Fever Syndrome.

Anyone with a shovel can dig a butter or a steamer clam, but it takes a sophisticated evolutionary tool kit to dig a razor clam. This is especially true in the night tides, where you must dodge the full fury of the Pacific surf in hopes of spotting the faintest dimple in the sand that reveals the presence of the elusive razor clam. Spotting the clam and digging them are two different things. Sometimes it's a challenge to match wits with a clam, until you remember they have no brain. When you find yourself kneeling on a tide flat in the dark with your arm in a hole in the sand feeling around for a clam, you realize you have been defeated and outsmarted by a creature with no central nervous system. That makes perfect sense in the evolutionary scheme of things. Bivalves have been around since the Cambrian Era more than five hundred million years ago. The whole time the clams have been evolving into stronger, smarter and faster organisms with complex abilities to survive in a hostile environment. Meanwhile humans seem to be evolving into a less intelligent creature with every passing year.

People have different theories on how to dig razor clams. Some use a shovel while others employ a clam gun. Both methods involve back-breaking labor. Razor clams move with surprising speed in wet sand by extending their foot or digger then flattening it out like an anchor. The clam pulls itself down to its anchor and repeats the process, digging down at a rate that is faster than some people can dig with a shovel given the conditions. Some clam diggers hunt razor clams on the dry tide flats and others look in the surf where the clams are shallow and easier to dig, in theory. As the wave retreats, you have only a little time before another wave crashes in. You must spot the clam and dig like a banshee with the roar of the surf at your back until you've dug as deep as you dare. Then you reach down into the dark, wet hole to grab the fleeing clam that is digging downward at a rate that is unbelievable to anyone but a clam digger. With any luck at all, you are able to grab the shell of the retreating clam, maybe with only a thumb and forefinger. There you struggle with the fleeing clam as it tries to dig to China. In the heat of the struggle, you hear another clam digger rush by, heading back toward the beach shouting,

"Wave!"

A decision must be made. Let go of the giant razor clam or hang on and get creamed by a wave of unknown height, bearing down on you in the night. At this point we may consider the effect of the Butterfly Theory. That the movement of the air caused by a butterfly flapping its wings in South America, could cause a hurricane in Texas. Similarly, a razor clam squirting on a beach in Alaska could produce a rogue wave on the coast of Washington. It's just a theory, but I was keeping an eye out for rogue waves all the same. They can be a hundred feet tall, sink the largest ship and ruin your clam dig. As the big wave came in, I hung on to that clam for dear life, hoping its anchor would hold us both. It did. I got my clam. I got my limit. I didn't have cabin fever anymore!

2

OLYMPIC MOUNTAIN GROUNDHOG DAY.

It was daylight on the water. A pounding hull in a rough sea told me what had happened. I'd been shanghaied, again. Through the murk of dawn, I saw bluffs that rose out of the sea on the port side and a narrow sand-spit closing the bay on the starboard. I shuddered; we were crossing the bar at the mouth of Sequim Bay.

This was the site of "Such-kwee-ing" the largest village of the S'Klallam nation. The village contained about a dozen split-cedar houses along the beach. The largest was the potlatch house owned by the chief, Xaiske'nim. A row of poles along the beach held the severed heads of enemies killed in war.

Sequim was said to be the S'Klallam word for "quiet waters," all of which means nothing when you're headed for the open sea into the teeth of a February Nor'easter that froze my brain to the marrow.

Shanghaiing was supposed to have died out years ago, but it didn't, picture bingo night at the lodge. I hadn't noticed how everyone else avoided the eggnog. I thought it meant more for me. The last thing I remember was the leering mug of Captain Carp just before the lights went out.

Carp was of a cutthroat fleet of Dungeness crabbers at war in the Strait of Juan de Fuca. He always seemed to need another deckhand. I had ignored the gossip that had been floating around for years, about him using deckhands for crab-bait. Once aboard it didn't take long to learn the truth: Carp would use his own mother-in-law for bait if he thought it would work.

I couldn't say just how long I was trapped on the boat. We were miles from shore. I missed my soap opera. After a while I started to notice we were getting low on bait.

"Nobody walks off this job," the captain chuckled as he hacked away at another tub of bait with a dull machete.

Some folks think crab like rotten stuff, and maybe they do, but it's best to use the freshest bait you can find if you're going to entice them into a trap. You want bait that's oily with a lot of aroma, which would have described me after a day on a crab boat.

I knew I had only one chance to get off that boat. I waited until after the grog ration and told Captain Carp about the best secret bait for crab in these waters: marmots. The marmots that infest the alpine regions of the Olympic Mountains are a unique species of mega-rodents that spend the short months of summer high in the alpine meadows picking flowers, raising their young and digging burrows where they sleep through the long night of winter.

While modern science continues to debate whether the Olympic Marmot attains a true state of hibernation like members of Congress, it is no wonder this iconic creature was chosen as the official Washington state mammal. Any creature that spends most of its life sleeping in a tunnel with no light at the end of it could serve as a role model for the rest of the citizens of our fair state.

It was this mountain lifestyle that I found so attractive. I spent years gaining the trust of the marmots. It is one of my proudest accomplishments, which involved discipline and a lot of hard work. First, I stopped bathing. Then I sat very still and grew my hair until I was furry enough to blend in with the marmots. Eventually I made friends with the marmots the old-fashioned way, grooming and posturing until I was accepted into enlarged portions of their dens.

There I was able to decipher much of the marmot language. The marmots communicate with a series of whistles that sound like a car alarm or make you think the police are coming. They whistle to warn each other of coyotes, eagles and that other backcountry pest, the waffle-stomping granola-crunching backpackers. These are people who carry big loads of expensive tents and gourmet freeze-dried food on their backs while wandering around pretending to be homeless.

The marmot language is easy to understand. They are making fun of us. Biologists thought the number of marmots in Olympic National Park could be depressed by anything from climate change to coyotes. If the marmots were depressed, they could be endangered. If they weren't endangered, they should be.

As a way of giving back, I volunteered to carry out a survey of the declining numbers of marmots. That was a difficult task since the marmots live underground most of the time. To get an accurate count of the marmots I took it upon myself to develop innovative survey techniques using zircon encrusted electrodes to run electricity down their holes and shock the marmots out into the open where they could be easily counted.

Since all marmots look pretty much the same, a methodology had to be developed to avoid counting the same marmot twice. At first it seemed like a good idea to paintball the marmots, but weapons are not allowed in Olympic National Park. Instead it was decided to shave a small portion of the marmot. Any marmot with a bad haircut meant it had been previously recorded in the survey.

Then we'd attach a radio collar with a webcam to the marmot and see if they could still fit back in their hole. This would unlock a treasure trove of data about the marmots' private lives that could make them the stars of their own reality TV show.

Potential marmot surveyor applicants had to be unemployed and able to fit into extremely small spaces for no pay. The Marmot Survey was looking for self-starting, out of the box team-players familiar with digging, blasting and mining techniques, with electroshocking and hair removal skills and able to pack extremely heavy loads through rugged terrain while blindfolded.

Marmot surveyors should celebrate the diversity of alternative camp styles, unlike the embittered marmot survey partner I was burdened with. We'll call him Edward. He was not a team player, saddled as he was with a 90-pound pack of freeze-dried this and light-weight that while I carried some Chinese take-out. Edward was just mad because I thought of it first. There is no room for haters on the Marmot Survey, not when the future of this iconic species depends on our survey efforts.

Unfortunately, the soulless automatons of the one-world-order-park rangers wouldn't let me onto the Olympic National Park Marmot Survey Team. Some sort of sissy wilderness safety rules prohibited marmot surveyors from surveying alone. Surveying marmots is like any other hunting trip. I hunt alone. When I hunt alone, I'd rather be by myself. It requires solitude to gain the animal's trust and get back to the burrow where the magic happens. Adding more surveyors to the mix can compromise the mission.

Just getting to marmot country is a challenge. I parked at the Dungeness Trail at daylight. Backpacking is a back-breaking form of strangulation that would be outlawed as torture by the Geneva Convention if not for the fact that you do it to yourself. As I made my way across the parking lot, I began to feel feverish, short of breath and dizzy as a tweaker in a crosswalk. Little did I suspect that thousands of feet beneath me a great tectonic struggle between the Juan de Fuca Plate and the North American Continent was forcing the Olympic Mountains even higher! No wonder I was exhausted! There was only one thing to do: cook some bacon. After that it was time to take a nap and bandage the blisters on my feet. Days later, with the expedition running seriously low on bacon, I reached marmot country, a place called Avalanche Valley.

I made my way to the head of the valley where a number of marmots whistled a cheery welcome.

I had just followed a marmot pretty far into its den when disaster struck. The Juan de Fuca Plate must have slipped against the leading edge of the continental shelf, again. I was stuck between two colliding tectonic plates of the Earth's crust with my head stuck in a marmot hole.

Then I was attacked by an aggressive marmot with its vicious fangs bared and its fur all turned the wrong way. It was whistling like a rabid pig, less than two feet from my face. That's the time when some marmot surveyors will panic, go claustrophobic and wash out of the marmot survey team. Our instructors had tried to prepare us for a confrontation like this during 'hell week' in marmot surveyor school, where we were locked in a 50-gallon drum and rolled down a steep hill.

Still, nothing can prepare you for getting trapped in an occupied marmot burrow. Things can get crazy fast and anything can happen. Being afraid of marmots is nothing to be ashamed of. It's how you handle that fear that determines your chances of survival as a marmot surveyor. Luckily it was a hot day and I was sweating bacon grease. Eventually I squeezed out of the hole and headed back down the mountain with my survey results. Park Service officials said they would preserve them in the appropriate file.

Years later, with Captain Carp running out of crab bait, I remembered the marmots. While I had taken the sacred oath of a marmot surveyor to never use my special knowledge for evil, it was me or the marmots. I had to think of something. I just sort of put two and two together and told the captain that in February, the marmots dig their way out of 20 feet of snow to check out their shadows. That's how they predict the coming of spring hereabouts. I assured Captain Carp that marmots were the best crab bait in these waters and I had a sure-fire method of catching them. All I needed was the right gear. Captain Carp dropped me ashore with a fish net and a gunny-sack. I escaped into the woods where I was able to write this.

3

VALENTINE'S DAY.

You don't see many women out on the river. Once in a while a guy will call up and want to take his wife on a winter steelhead fishing trip. That's when I ask, "Have you tried counseling?"

Married people should try a less drastic solution than steelhead fishing, before their relationship reaches a point of no return. Sometimes by reminding them of feelings they might have had before marriage, the couple will come to their senses and realize that no steelhead is worth risking a relationship. I've heard all the excuses. Money, power, revenge, but that's still no excuse to subject your significant other to the pain and abuse of a winter steelhead fishing trip where even the fish are too cold to wiggle. Steelhead fishing can destroy relationships.

I know that now, after the way my heart got stomped by that waitress. She had pretty hair. She worked in a bistro slinging steaks cut from cows that must have limped off the Ark. There was watery coffee in dirty cups. She yelled at me for being a worthless fisherman and tracking my muddy boots across the floor. I wasn't there for the food. I was homesick.

I remember the good times. There was the secret glance that was like the recoil of a .338 Winchester magnum shooting a 300-grain bullet pushing 3,000 foot/pounds or so. There was the hidden gesture and the five-dollar bill I gave her for putting a shot of dish soap in that bragging fly fisherman's coffee. Before I knew it, I started hanging around the grease fryer. I fantasized about us running off to a plunking bar with a jug of pickled herring. I knew it was wrong to fall in love with the waitress the minute she mentioned her husband.

"He's so stupid and lazy," my dream-boat purred. "I have to tape a can of beer to the lawnmower just to get him to push it around." Why are all the good ones taken? I had too much respect for the marriage institution to ever want "shot by a jealous husband" on my headstone. I can only counsel that we all handle rejection with a good helping of sensitivity and maturity that allows a certain degree of personal growth from the experience. That must be why I locked myself in the restroom, turned on the hot water and let the cares of the world run down the drain no matter how long they beat on the door.

Then I got a call about a fishing trip. She said she was a kickboxing instructor from east Athabasca. She could karate chop my heart right out of my chest so I could watch it beat while I died. That kind of thing could come in handy out on the river. She wanted to book a fishing trip. I tried to talk her out of it but she showed up to go fishing anyway. At least my conscience was clear, for a while. Do you believe in love at first sight? I'm certain it happens all the time. She had pretty hair. I launched the boat, rowed downriver and got the gear working. It was one of those clear February days you wait for all winter. When the river drops from gray to blue we catch the biggest steelhead of the year. Eagles soared through a cloudless sky. The snow-capped Olympic Mountains seemed near enough to touch. It was "fish on!" almost immediately.

It was almost a perfect day of fishing, except for one thing. My guts began to churn and howl like an alien was trying to crawl out. Then I remembered: We'd stopped at "Soapy's" for breakfast. I noticed that two-timing waitress laughing in the back with the fly fisherman. It all added up. I'd been soaped!

After some agonizing hours, it was lunch time. The kickboxer offered me a sandwich. It looked about the size of a bale of hay, with bacon, egg and yellow cheese all frozen together in a lump. I couldn't say no. I said I'd love a sandwich.

"Look, there's an eagle," I said. When she turned to look, I chucked the sandwich in the river. That's when the nightmare began. For whatever reason, maybe because it was frozen, the sandwich wouldn't sink. It began floating along with the boat. It kept up right through the riffles, sticking out of the water like a little shark fin.

The rest of the day was a stomach-churning memory. We caught a lot of steelhead, just how many, I was in too much agony to say, but it was one of those days. You could spend the rest of your life on the river and never have another one like it. I told her she should probably never go steelhead fishing again. She didn't.

VALENTINE'S DAY – POLLY.

When I first met Polly, I could tell she'd been around. She had a few miles on her. She was shacked up with a logger – not that there's anything wrong with that. He used to take her fishing on the weekends during what they call the honeymoon stage. It didn't take too long before the honeymoon was over. The log market must have got hot or his interest must have cooled because the next thing you know she was staying home every weekend while he was out logging with his buddies.

That doesn't work in any relationship, and maybe I shouldn't have gotten involved in the first place. I just wanted to go fishing without the chaos, guilt and drama that can ruin a good trip.

My previous relationship had been on the rocks so often it left me with a sinking feeling that we were going under. Sure, any relationship involves a lot of hard work to maintain an even keel, but at the end of the day it's about quality time and having fun. I'm not the bad guy here. The fact is Polly went fishing with me and I'm not going to say I'm sorry. There is no looking back. Life happens. And when it happens, it's better to just sit back and go for the ride instead of placing blame, pointing fingers and asking a lot of pointless questions that have no answer.

It really is about all the small pieces that come together to complete the puzzle. I know it sounds corny and I probably shouldn't even be writing this, so if you don't like reading mushy stuff about a guy being in love, you should stop reading this right now.

All I can say is that some things are meant to happen. I knew that the minute I slipped the tongue of her trailer on my tow ball. It was exactly the right size. She even had a compatible four-pronged wiring harness that fit together perfectly with mine. All I had to do was flip the switch and her tail lights lit up my world.

I'll never forget our first fishing trip. You can find out a lot about a personality out on the river in a real hurry. There is not time to pussy foot or beat around the bush. You can either handle yourself on the water or you can't. Polly could. I learned a lot about Polly on that first trip. All I had to do was put the rod in her holder and that rod would go off. It was amazing. Traditionally boats were named for a benevolent goddess or the captain's mother or wife. Polly was short for the polyester resin she was made with, the pure virgin extract of fossilized dinosaurs.

As with any relationship there was a period of adjustment. I'll admit I screwed up by taking Polly out at Oil City one Saturday night. The place was like Sodom and Gomorrah with a hangover. I almost lost her. There was a lot of tension at the boat ramp and something snapped. Polly slid down the bank and out into the Hoh River like a runaway party barge. She was headed for the open ocean to be cast up by the surf on a lonely wilderness beach then flown out by the Coast Guard as part of a trash removal exercise in the spring. She deserved better. I waded out in the river in the dark and rescued her.

I tried to just remember the good times. But sometimes the good times aren't enough. I hit her with rocks. I always said I was sorry and it would never happen again, but it did happen, again and again. I was ashamed. After a while her bottom started to leak. People started talking, saying I should get a new boat. No way. We patched things up. Polly and I are on the water again with a wild joy in our heartstrings.

5

APRIL FOOL'S DAY.

April Fool's Day often brings to mind a dreadful series of frightful practical jokes played upon the hapless inmates of a remote fish camp located somewhere in a distant corner of the rainforest. It was here the childish antics of a few ruined an otherwise pristine nature experience for the rest, causing questions to be asked: Who replaced the sugar with borax? Who put the pickled herring juice in the pancake syrup? Who left the carton of sand shrimp, the fastest rotting substance known to science, under the seat of my truck?

It was a mistake to choke down the borax flavored pancakes smothered in pickled herring syrup. It might have clogged my gizzard. I thought I was off my feed, so I tried washing it down with some hot coffee that had been surreptitiously seasoned with enough cayenne pepper to melt a railroad spike. It was then I noticed someone had set my boots on fire. By then I was crying uncle. If revenge is a dish best served cold, it could take years to get even but I will.

Curiously, the most fiendishly cruel practical joke I ever heard of was not performed by some anonymous drunken fisherman but by a government bureaucracy that we have no possibility of ever getting even with. You probably thought the state of Washington was run by a power-mad cabal of self-serving, pencil-pushing, pocket-lining functionaries whose only purpose is to make our lives miserable. You didn't know that the government also has a keen sense of humor, irony and revenge, but they do. Why else would they insist that we get our new fishing license on April Fool's Day?

The money from fishing license sales goes to support many worthwhile government programs like, the advanced, state-of-the-art computer systems that are required to administer fishing license sales. Fishing license sales also provide vital funding for the latest scientific research that might someday allow the state to design a punch card the average angler can figure out. The punch cards are a vital part of the Fish Cop Employment Security Act, which allows them the opportunity to write tickets at almost any time, anywhere.

The law says you are to immediately record your catch on the punch card in ink, with the catch and location code. For the steelhead angler, this can be a real challenge. While it is true that most of the fishing on the Olympic Peninsula is done on bar stools or at the day job where the one that got away fish fables flow freely, much of the local angling effort is conducted on or near the water where it is possible or even likely that the swimsuit region of the angler which would most likely contain the license and punch cards that we all must carry, will be exposed to water. The ink used to print your punch card is not waterproof.

Imagine standing in a freezing river in leaking boots in a blizzard. You were lucky enough to catch a steelhead. You must fill out your punch card. First you must find a pen. This could involve an extensive search of your pockets, which is difficult when your hands are so cold they have lost all feeling. By the time you have found a pen, your exposed punch card has gotten wet. All of the ink has washed off leaving you with a blank piece of paper. Getting the ink to stick to the paper can be as difficult as hooking a steelhead. You could try to write the name of the river to record your catch, but that would be too easy. Instead there is a secret code for each river buried in the depths of the 150-page fishing rules pamphlet. By now your pen is frozen. You try to thaw the pen, but this is difficult because your fingers are frozen. You try to write the name of the river on the blank piece of paper that used to be a punch card and end up with something that looks like an ink blob.

Filling out a salmon punch card is no picnic either. Imagine bouncing in a heavy swell out in the salt-chuck while trying to fight down a force-10 case of sea-sickness. You catch a salmon anyway. The salmon punch card requires you to determine what species you caught along with whether the fish has a clipped fin or not. Determining the species of a salmon can be as difficult as catching one. With blurred vision and a shaking hand, you scribble something on your punch card that looks like an ink blob.

Filling out a crab punch card should be easy, but it is not. Imagine wading out to the top of your boots to try to scoop up a crab. Just as you grab your crab, some joker in a power boat roars by at top speed sending a tsunami-sized wake your way. You, your punch card and your pen are now soaked in salt water. You eventually smear an ink blob on your punch card.

Theoretically the punch cards are returned to the state bean counters, who interpret the meaning of the ink blobs with a secret method not unlike the interpretation of the Rorschach test. Have a happy April Fool's Day! Why not; the joke is on you.

6

NATIONAL PET DAY – APRIL 11 – BEST FISHING BUDDY.

Pardon me for being a little down. You can get that way losing a fishing buddy. He was the best ever. Over the years, he saw it all, from 30-pound steelhead to 50-pound king salmon, but there's more to fishing the rivers of the rainforest than catching fish. It requires teamwork, communication and balance. Without these things, the vessel will lose control and bad things can happen. You need someone aboard who can keep their head about them when all others have lost their fragile grip, someone who can serve as a shining beacon to humanity. That he was. I'll never forget the first fishing trip we went on. At first, I thought it was more than a little weird he didn't have a fishing pole, but what the heck, I provide all the gear. Then I found out he didn't have a fishing license or a punch-card. That was a red flag. Our fish cops are meaner than pepper-sprayed protesters. Fishing without a fishing license is a violation that can get you a big ticket. I said right off that the big guy wasn't fishing, but everyone said that was OK because he just wanted to ride along and have some snacks.

"Snacks?" I asked and sure enough the big guy had a whole bag of bacon flavored snacks that looked like little sausages, yum. Everyone piled in the boat. The snacks were running low by the time we hooked a fish. Then it was one fish after another until we limited out. Through it all, the big guy just sat there cool as a cucumber taking in the scenery, which was pretty remarkable considering we just had a triple-header hook-up on steelhead. Typically, a steelhead will jump in circles around the boat. With three fish on at once, the three guys that were hooked up were jumping in circles around the boat. That's while spinning in circles down the river.

"Why don't you get the big guy a fishing license? We could still be fishing," I sobbed.

"They won't let him have a fishing license," my fancy friend said. I was shocked. I thought discrimination was a part of our ugly past that had been laid to rest long ago, that we celebrate diversity in all its forms and treat everyone as an equal. It was then I knew it was time for this wilderness gossip columnist to get down in the trenches and do some investigative journalism. I discovered a systematic pattern of discrimination still being practiced by the Washington state Department of Fish and Wildlife. They claim to not discriminate on the basis of race or gender, but what good is that if they won't issue a fishing license to a Labrador retriever? Dogs are man's oldest friend. They have been fishing as long as man has. To deny a fishing dog like Boone a fishing license is a blot on the soul of a corrupt regime.

Boone was never bitter about it. He learned to cope with prejudice and bigotry with grace and style. Some dogs have owners, Boone had a staff. He let us catch and cook the fish for him, with bacon of course. Boone seemed so young when he passed, just 13 years old. The good really do die young. There's no way to make sense of it. We figured the good Lord just needed a fishing dog more than we did.

7

EARTH DAY.

I remember the first Earth Day. It was back in 1970. Fishing must have been slow because I was in school. They herded us into a big hall and showed us a film about how we were killing the Earth with pollution. That was good news to us. Up until then we thought the Earth was going to get blown up in the nuclear war we were always practicing for. In the event of a nuclear attack, we were all to climb under our desks. Just how we were going to survive an atomic bomb that would melt a battleship by climbing under the desk was anyone's guess but we were all for anything that got us out of class. I thought school was a complete waste of time if we were all just going to get blown up anyway. We should have been building the bomb shelter that belonged in every American home. When they dropped the big one we could sit inside drinking barrels of war surplus water and chow down on K-rations until the radiation cooled in 10,000 years or so, while the rest of the losers beat on the door to let them in. But we wouldn't.

Little did I suspect at the time what killing the Earth would do to the fishing. Fishing was terrific back on the first Earth Day. That old pioneer saying about walking across the creek on the backs of the salmon was still true. Since then people have been wondering. What happened to the fish?

Shortly after the first Earth Day, the historic Boldt Decision gave the treaty tribes of Washington the right to half of the harvestable fish.

Under the terms of the Boldt Decision, if either the tribes, commercial or sport fishing fleet failed to harvest its share of the fish, the other side could. This set off a fish war where both sides of the dispute tried to kill the last fish. Within a few short years, it seemed like giving the treaty tribes half the fish was like giving them half of the buffalo. The extinction of the salmon represents the elimination of a biomass greater than the sixty million bison that used to roam North America. The salmon have been pushed to the brink of extinction by a new form of pollution that was never mentioned at the first Earth Day, nylon pollution. Most fishing line is made out of nylon. Gill nets, trawl nets, drift nets and sport fishermen's landing nets are all made out of nylon. There's just too much nylon in the water for the fish to survive.

Nylon pollution affects the fish before they are born. Male and female salmon and steelhead pair up to dig a nest in the gravel, in which to bury the fertilized eggs. The nest is called a redd. Fisheries biologists love to count redds. It's a scientific method of counting your eggs before they are hatched. They call it a management tool. Once identified as a shallow depression of freshly turned gravel, the redd surveyors will drop or pound a metal spike covered with plastic ribbons into the nest. How would you like someone dumping a load of garbage in your bed? Well the fish don't like it any better. They abandon redds treated in this manner. Redd surveyors love flagging the streamside bushes with plastic ribbons. This ugly reminder of fisheries mismanagement tells any passing angler where the spawning fish lie. The markers are a free streamside guide to anyone who wants to stomp the eggs into the gravel or snag the spawners off their beds. Just look for the tangle of plastic ribbons to find the fish.

Once the baby fish hatch, they face many dangers in their life's journey, starting with the smolt trap. A smolt is a baby fish that's migrating downstream to the ocean. A smolt trap can block the entire width of a small stream. This stops the upstream spring migration of other fish, like the sea-run cutthroat and steelhead, for weeks at a time. It allows an opportunity for the bull trout and cutthroat to get into the smolt trap and eat the baby fish that are trapped there. Otters, mink and bears can get into the smolt traps to eat the bull trout and cutthroat. Floods can wash the smolt traps out into the woods. All this rough handling occurs at a critical time when the smolts are about to miraculously transform themselves from a fresh to a saltwater fish. If they survive the smolt trap, the fish can make their way to the open ocean where the real danger lies. The trawl fleet or draggers accidentally catches thousands of salmon every year while targeting other species. There are miles of nylon drift nets, purse seine nets, gill nets, a trolling fleet and the landing nets of the sport anglers each fighting the other for their share of the kill.

All fishermen eventually lose some gear. Lost nets do not stop fishing. They are called ghost nets. They sink and snag up on the rocks where every sort of sea creature, including crab, salmon, ling cod, seals, sea lions, porpoises and sea birds, can become entangled in a swirling mass of nylon and rotting sea creatures, all victims of nylon pollution.

Eventually the salmon that survive the nylon pollution in the ocean can return to their home rivers. First, they have to swim upstream through another maze of nylon, the tribal gill nets located at the mouth of every river. The survivors are targeted by sport anglers who will fish the salmon clear back upriver to the redds completing the cycle of nylon pollution.

Nylon pollution is only one of many new forms of pollution that have been discovered since the first Earth Day. Every year 97,000 pounds of drugs, hormones and personal care product residues that are pumped into Puget Sound by 106 publicly owned wastewater treatment plants. The chemicals are not monitored, regulated or removed from wastewater. Scientists found an alphabet soup of chemical residues in the tissues of young salmon that had to swim through the wastewater. That could explain why these young fish have such a hard time migrating out to the big world and becoming adults. Experiments with juvenile humans have shown that exposure to these same chemicals, which include nicotine, caffeine, OxyContin, Paxil, Valium, Zoloft and cocaine, can produce the similar results. These substances are called "chemicals of concern" since their effect on fish and human growth, behavior, reproduction and immune function is unknown. We don't know at what levels these chemicals are present in adult fish. We don't know the effect on marine mammals that eat fish but those at the top of the food chain, like humans, would be the most vulnerable. The side-effects of chemical experiments on self-medicating human subjects are well documented, producing a myriad of anti-social and evolutionary dead-end behaviors from raiding the fridge to robbing the liquor store. The potential dangers of a coked-up killer whale or a sea lion on an OxyContin binge should be fairly obvious.

Traveling west of Puget Sound, we find Hood Canal. This magnificent glacial fiord was once the most productive marine environment in the Pacific Northwest, with an inexhaustible bounty of oysters, clams, shrimp, crab, salmon and bottom fish. This Earth Day finds Hood Canal turning into a watery dead zone from a lack of oxygen. We are studying the problem. Traveling west of Hood Canal, we come to Dungeness Bay, home of the famous Dungeness crab. Back during the first Earth Day, you could fish for spring chinook salmon, soak a crab pot and dig some clams. Since that first Earth Day, the oysters and clams of Dungeness Bay were polluted, and the king salmon and steelhead are endangered. The Dungeness River, famous for having the best spring steelhead fishing in the state of Washington, is now closed to fishing for most of the year.

Continuing west from Dungeness Bay we come to Port Angeles. Its' harbor was polluted by pulp mills, sewage and log-handling scraps since long before the first Earth Day. The harbor and areas downwind contain unknown quantities of dioxins and other pollutants that we are studying in hopes of cleaning it up someday.

Continuing west of Port Angeles on our Earth Day tour, we come to the largest and most significant man-made structure on the Olympic Peninsula: Mount Trashmore, a giant mountain of garbage at the Port Angeles Landfill. In the bad old days before the first Earth Day, we threw our garbage off a cliff into the eternal flames of burning trash on the edge of the Strait of Juan de Fuca. Later we buried the garbage until we couldn't bury it anymore so we piled it up in a mountain until we decide what to do with it.

West of Mount Trashmore, we come to ground zero for the biggest environmental movement the Olympic Peninsula has ever seen: the removal of the Elwha River dams. The Spanish explorer Manuel Quimper said he bought some 100-pound salmon from the Indians off the mouth of the Elwha back in July of 1790. Quimper could not keep his mouth shut. People have been coming to fish the Elwha ever since. The Elwha Dam and the Glines Canyon Dam were built without any way for the fish to get over them in 1913 and 1927. Blocking a salmon stream was illegal at the time but then as now there were ways of getting around the law. These illegal dams on the Elwha were blamed for killing off the fish. It's strange however, for salmon that only live three to six years were abundant in the Elwha decades after the dams were built.

In October 1945, Port Angeles Evening News editor Jack Henson, known as "The Wandering Scribe," described the Elwha 30 years after the Elwha Dam was built as the "Valhalla of the spring (king) salmon." Henson found these "monarchs of the salt-chuck by the hundreds fulfilling their ultimate destiny of spawning and dying to perpetuate their race."

All I know is if I could have been skipping school during that first Earth Day, I would have fished the Elwha. It was one of the top steelhead rivers in Washington at the time. Why did it take decades for the Elwha fish to became endangered and/or extinct species? Was there something even more deadly than an impassable dam that killed off the fish?

The Elwha and the Queets rivers flow like twins from opposite sides of the Olympic Mountains, but their history could not be more different. The Elwha was blocked by an impassable dam. Its waters siphoned off for industrial use, its fish caught in such terrific numbers they rotted on the cannery docks. The Queets remained "terra incognita" until 1890 when the U.S. Army sent Lt. Joseph P. O'Neil and his mule trains to climb the Olympics and bring back a map. A member of O'Neil's expedition, Harry Fisher, became lost after climbing Mount Olympus on Sept. 20, 1890 and wandered down the Queets River. Fisher reported that sleeping along the Queets was like "a camp in Barnum's Menagerie as far as sleep was concerned." Between the thrashing of the salmon in the river and the breaking of brush by the large animals hunting the salmon, he had a hard time sleeping.

On Sept. 26, Private Fisher was hailed by an Indian who had the same name and offered a canoe ride down-river. Fisher describes the Native American method of taking salmon in a weir and hitting the fish at 20 or 30 feet with a forked spear. His host had speared six large salmon and quit fishing. Fisher describes his "staunch friend" watching the many splashing salmon with "Pride, as a farmer would his cattle."

The Queets was never dammed. It is a pristine habitat protected within a national park that allows only catch and release fishing for native species of salmon, trout and steelhead. Still the Queets fish are considered threatened or endangered. What happened to the Queets fish that made them as rare as the fish in the Elwha? Scientists predict the removal of the Elwha dams will restore the historic run of 400,000 salmon and steelhead that will be able to spawn in the miles of pristine habitat above the dams. It makes you wonder why the scientists can't restore rivers like the Queets, Quinault, Hoh, Quileute and all the many smaller rivers and creeks that flow through a pristine habitat and have never been dammed. Maybe it's something in the water that's killing the fish, besides all the nylon pollution and sewage.

In her 1962 book "Silent Spring," Rachel Carson wrote about the effects of the myriad hazardous chemicals wantonly sprayed in the environment. Carson said DDT, 24D and 2-4-5-T were, "As crude a weapon as any cave man's club, the chemical barrage has been hurled against the fabric of life." Rachel Carson died before the first Earth Day. By then the Olympic Peninsula was being sprayed with 24D along power lines to clear the lines and in clear-cuts to kill alders and anything else that would compete with the Douglas fir seedlings. People spraying these chemicals and industry scientists assured us the stuff did not persist in the environment, it just dried up and disappeared. In fact, it was claimed to be so harmless they could drink the herbicides with no ill effects.

When the effect of Agent Orange, an herbicide whose key ingredient was 24D, on returning Vietnam veterans was finally recognized by the U.S. government we learned that the key to understanding science was to learn who was paying the scientist. Since the first Earth Day we have sprayed the alders to get rid of them or any other vegetation that is not a Douglas fir seedling, despite the fact that alder has become more valuable than the Douglas fir. Industry propagandists have invented new "harmless" chemicals and reasons for spraying them. Clear-cuts are sprayed with herbicides to kill what is called "pre-emergent growth" that is anything besides the planted seedlings. Even the environmental movement has embraced the use of chemicals. Claiming invasive plants harm salmon, government sponsored environmental organizations spray herbicides along our rivers as an excuse for salmon restoration.

There is no point in asking the question: what happened to the fish? Given the way we have mismanaged and polluted our fisheries since the first Earth Day the question is: why is there one fish left?

8

ARBOR DAY – THE GRANDFATHER TREE.

It was daylight in the swamp a thousand years ago. In a tree on the uphill edge of the meadow, a Douglas squirrel sat on a limb shelling a fir cone. Her cheeks were stuffed so full of seeds she didn't see the great white goshawk drop like a thunderbolt. The fir cone fell to the ground in a pile of shelled seeds. Many of the seeds were eaten by mice. The rest sprouted in a tangle of seedlings. Some of the seedlings grew faster than others in a race to the sun. The smaller seedlings were crowded out until rabbits and deer came through and nipped the buds off the tops of the taller ones. The survivors grew quickly on the edge of the open meadow. One autumn a large herd of elk passed through. The bulls used the little fir grove to strip the velvet off their antlers. One of the trees was ripped out of the ground. Others had their tops broken and bark stripped. Only a couple of the little trees survived the carnage unhurt.

That spring a black bear came by as the sap began to flow. The bear was hungry for the cambium layer just beneath the outer bark of the fir. The bear peeled the bark off one of the trees from the ground to its crown then slid down the trunk, breaking limbs as he fell. The bear had just slashed a wound in the remaining fir when something caused him to stop and smell the wind.

There was the smell of man and his ally, fire. Some men had set fire to the meadow in an effort to attract game to the fresh growth after the burn. The dry grass went up in a ball of smoke and flame.

The fire singed the bark of the fir and cauterized the wound from the bear. The tree survived the fire and tried to heal itself. Fresh bark grew over the burn but the scars from the bear would not heal. The tree grew around the wound until there formed a hollow that grew with the tree. As the centuries passed, different animals took shelter in the hollow of the grandfather tree. One fall just before a big snowstorm, a bear enlarged the hollow for a den to spend the winter in. Another century passed. A mother cougar used the cave to raise a litter of kittens. One evening just before dark, an Indian boy crouched before the tree, kindling a small fire that he fed through the night. He prayed, fasted and waited for his guardian spirit to appear.

A century passed before another man came along. This one had a light complexion and a beard. He had jumped from a ship and escaped into the woods with a rifle, powder and lead, flint and steel. He knew the captain would pay the Indians to catch him and bring him back to the ship where he would be whipped and chained in a rat-infested hold. The natives were a rough bunch with skulls on poles in front of their houses. The sailor thought if he could hide until the ship went away, the Indians would be more reasonable. He could teach them the use of gunpowder if it came to that.

Half a century passed. One day a man chopped a blaze into the side of the tree. This marked the corner of a homestead claim the man could own if he could build a cabin and a garden before winter. The fastest way to clear ground in this country was to start a stump fire. One spring the stump fire got away into the surrounding forest. The thick bark of the grandfather tree was burned black. The homesteaders went to work amid the burnt stumps. Soon there was a tidy farm of split cedar shacks with gardens of hay, oats and potatoes.

A half a century passed. There was a Great Depression that crippled the entire country. Most of the homesteads were abandoned. The hayfields and gardens sprouted a thick new crop of fir seedlings that grew in the shadow of the grandfather tree.

Another half a century passed. The young firs grew into trees the size of cabin logs. There came the sound of a chainsaw. A logger was cutting the second growth. He stopped for water at the grandfather tree. It was hollow and twisted, scarred and burned but still alive.

"Leave 'er stand," the logger said as he moved on to face up a cut on another tree. The squirrels ran ahead of the falling trees. One of them stopped on a limb to shell a fir cone. It did not see the white goshawk, dropping to earth like a thunderbolt.

9

ARBOR DAY – THE GRANDMOTHER TREE.

It was daylight in the swamp, 750 years before the present. A strong wind had been blowing since midnight. It whipped the crowns of the hemlocks until they groaned with the agony of trying to stay connected to the earth. Limbs, tops and slabs of loose bark from dead snags cut loose and flew through the air to crash on the ground. One tree fell and then another, shaking the swamp with the impact of many tons of wood returning to the earth. Then the wind died. By evening the swamp was a silent scene of devastation. Trees were stacked like pick-up sticks piled one atop the other many feet in the air. Somewhere beneath these acres of piled up wood a small cedar tree saw the full light of day for the first time.

Though cedars can grow in the darkness of the forest floor, they do better in full sunlight. After the big blow, the little tree grew faster than it ever had before. It had a big head start on the rest of the seedlings that sprouted from the bark of the fallen trees. The downed wood had become nurse-logs for a new generation of trees.

In 20 years, the seedlings covered the blow downs with an impenetrable mat of new growth. The cedar stood above the other trees. It grew quickly in the thick mulch of downed wood that rotted back to earth. In 100 years, the cedar was two feet in diameter and 100 feet tall. One morning in the spring of the year there was a knocking sound of stone striking wood. A woman chipped a horizontal gash with a stone ax about a third of the way around the tree. She peeled back a section of bark to reveal the yellow sapwood beneath. The sap was running. When the woman pulled back, the bark slipped easily from the cedar, 5, 10, 20 feet in the air until the sheet broke loose and fell to the ground. The woman separated the bark into thin layers, rolled it into a bundle and packed it back to camp.

The camp itself was made of cedar boards, split from a log with elk-horn wedges, tied to a pole frame with rope made of twisted cedar bark. The canoes were made of cedar hollowed from logs then steamed with water and hot rocks until they were stretched to a graceful shape that looked like the hull of a clipper ship. The larger canoes were used for whaling. Cedar limbs were woven into ropes to secure the whale once it had been stuck with mussel-shell harpoons. The clothes of the people were made from the cedar bark that was dried and pounded and woven into cloth. Cedar roots were woven into baskets that were so water tight they could be used for cooking. The needles on the cedar limbs were used as medicine until the new diseases came that no medicine could cure. Then the forest was devoid of people. The cedar grew around the scar where the bark had been stripped while the center began to rot. Carpenter ants found the rotten wood and bored into the tree, making their home in a series of tunnels. Sawdust from the worker ants poured out of the holes to land in little piles on the forest floor. The pileated woodpecker came hunting the ants. It chopped big holes in the cedar that the other birds used to nest in.

One morning there was a new sound in the forest, of sharpened steel raking soft wood. Two small figures stood at the base of the cedar, pulling on a misery whip, a crosscut saw with wooden handles at either end. The fallers worked on the undercut, chopping a wagon load of chips with their double-bitted axes. Then they started sawing the back cut. The cedar groaned as it slowly began to topple then crashed to the earth in a tangle of broken limbs. The men went to work on the downed tree, bucking it into four-foot lengths then splitting the logs with steel wedges. The cedar blocks were split into boards and nailed in an overlapping fashion to a pole frame to form the walls and roof of a cabin. With the cabin finished, the homesteaders went to work on a barn for the livestock and hay. They built a smokehouse, a root cellar and fences, all of split cedar. In the space of a lifetime the farm was abandoned. Eventually the cabin roof caved in, leaving the walls to rot away. There in the duff where the cabin stood, a small cedar began to grow.

10

ARBOR DAY – HOW MUCH WOOD DOES A MAN NEED? WITH APOLOGIES TO TOLSTOY'S HOW MUCH LAND DOES A MAN NEED?

A man and his wife lived on a small farm in the backwoods of the Olympic Peninsula. If you were to ask what they raised on this farm, the answer would be obvious: firewood. There were woodpiles stacked between the fence posts, under trees and in sheds. One night after a hard day of woodcutting the man was on the back porch sharpening his chain saw.

"How much wood does a man need?" his wife asked.

"We need as much as we can get," the husband said. "And besides, it ain't like the stuff goes bad. You want to cure it for a couple of years to keep from getting a chimney fire."

The woman had heard this before. She walked quietly back inside, leaving him to explain his love of cutting firewood. How the energy of the sun was transformed through the miracle of photosynthesis into a plant that made wood and oxygen, a gas we used to burn the wood and release the heat of the sun in winter. How he loved the feel of a sharp saw cutting into a windfall at daylight. The windfalls and snags were no good for lumber anyway. He told of the bugs getting into down logs about as soon as they hit the ground and how the government's trying to shut down the honest firewood-cutters. They push perfectly good wood in a pile and cover it with plastic to burn and pollute the air.

The next day the man drove his truck far into the forest following fresh tracks of a log truck. He knew the spoor would lead him to a logging show that might take pity on a firewood-cutter with a cooler full of beer and smoked salmon jerky at quitting time. Sure enough, just past the fork in the road and around the bend the man found a high lead logging show set up in the middle of the road. With the beer and smoked salmon jerky the woodcutter made a deal with the loggers. They said the woodcutter could have all the wood he could cut in one day for free. Anything left would be torched by the government do-gooders just like a Third World slash burn.

The woodcutter barely slept that night. He had a nightmare of the loggers laughing around a bonfire made from the wood he cut. The next morning found him in the woods at first light with a "hot saw" he had borrowed from his brother-in-law. It was a souped-up chainsaw with oversized everything, no safety features and a three-foot bar. He figured he'd need a big saw for some of the pumpkin logs he rubber-necked the day before.

The big saw roared to life at the third pull. He started cutting through a big chunk of old growth fir like it was melted butter. The log was so big he would have to split the rounds into smaller pieces to move them to the road. None of that mattered as a stream of aromatic sawdust poured out of the saw, like water from a hose. He ran the saw until the sun was high in the sky. He started splitting the firewood and throwing it into the road. Towards afternoon it became obvious the man would have to really hustle to get all the wood he cut on the road by dark. As the sun dropped to the horizon, he kept finding more wood to cut.

Just at sunset, he felt faint and keeled over dead on the woodpile, where the loggers found him the next morning. How much wood does a man need? It turned out it was just enough to make the box to bury him in.

THE FIRST SALMON CEREMONY.

The story of the First Salmon Ceremony goes back to the melting of the continental ice sheet about 15,000 years ago, when the rivers we have today were formed. Salmon colonized the ice-free streams somewhere around 9,000 years ago. Sometime after that people began celebrating the yearly arrival of the salmon. The First Salmon Ceremony is the oldest community celebration in the Pacific Northwest. The First Salmon Ceremony was practiced in one form or another by people who lived in the range of the salmon from California to Alaska and east to the Continental Divide to appreciate the salmon. It was witnessed by members of the Lewis and Clark Expedition at a Skilloot village at the Dalles on the Columbia River on April 19, 1806. Captain Clark observed: "The whole village was rejoicing today over having caught a single salmon, which was considered as the harbinger of vast quantities in four or five days. In order to hasten the arrival of the salmon, the Indians, according to custom, dressed the fish and cut it into small pieces, one of which was given to every child in the village."

The First Salmon Ceremony is one of the oldest expressions of human faith, where the salmon are thanked for returning to the river. In the beginning the creator called all the creatures together and asked for a gift from each of them to help the humans survive. The first to come forward was the salmon. Believed to be immortal, the salmon lived in human form at the bottom of the ocean, in separate houses each according to their kind under the rule of a benevolent salmon king. Every year the king would order the salmon people to clothe themselves in salmon robes and go up rivers to reproduce themselves and offer their bodies as a voluntary sacrifice as food for the people, the animals and the forest. To thank the salmon people, the first salmon caught in the river each year was treated as a special guest. The meat was shared. The remains carefully returned to the river. It was believed that as long as the salmon were treated with respect, their bones washed and returned to the river; the fish would run forever. All of which might go a long way to explain the crummy fishing lately.

Then, for the first time in history, the Hoh River was closed to catching salmon for the entire summer. Imagine someone coming to your town and shutting down your grocery store, church, playground and drum circle. The Hoh River was all of those things. The scientists said the multi-million-dollar log jams all chained together with steel I-beams pounded into the bed of the Hoh River would bring the salmon back but they didn't. I guess fish don't grow on trees or fake log jams.

It was thought that by showing the salmon a new appreciation with a First Salmon Celebration, they would return. This was not a dog-friendly venue. The First Salmon would be offended if a dog came near them or ate any part of his body. I was secretly relieved. Cooking over a camp fire can be a challenge even without a snarling pack of dogs with questionable bathroom habits. People showed up with meat and fowls and vegetables, which I was expected to cook over a campfire since there were no salmon. I was skewering a kebab when the first dogs showed up. They ranged from the size of a small coyote to a small ox. The dogs' owners or human companions as they are known these days, all insisted their animal companions didn't bite or fight. This was true; they just growled and snapped while trying to barge into my experimental kitchen.

"Just kick the dog if it gets in the way," a human companion insisted. Why would I want to hurt my foot kicking a drooling beast that weighs almost as much as I do? The human companions kept a constant stream of instructions to the animal companions, yelling, "Come here! Go away!" while asking the animal companion rhetorical questions like, "How many times have I told you not to do that?" Then insisting, "You know better than that."

It's been said that a wet dog is the friendliest creature on Earth. Dogs are even friendlier when they get wet, roll in the sand and look for a place to shake it off. After the sandy barbecue, the elders told their stories of what the river used to be like. The First Salmon Ceremony became the No Salmon Ceremony. It was a celebration of life for the river and the salmon. Both of them were dead. It was all so depressing I got a puppy.

12

THE SKUNK CABBAGE FESTIVAL.

"Why did you have the Skunk Cabbage Festival?" a disgusted festival-goer asked after the fireworks were over and only the smoke remained. It's always easy to find fault and criticize when things go wrong. It was just another of many failed attempts to celebrate a piece of this little green paradise we call home. The Skunk Cabbage Festival was born from the altruistic ideal that having a week with no community festival on the Olympic Peninsula is an un-American affront to the very ideals that make this country so cool. Community festivals give towns a sense of their rich history to pass on to future generations. For example, the Port Townsend Wooden Boat Festival celebrates America's maritime heritage in a town full of environmentalists who want to ban logging the trees that are required to make the lumber to build wood boats. The Sequim Irrigation Festival celebrates the invention of the irrigation ditch. The Forks Old Fashioned Fourth of July hearkens back to a simpler time when loggers ruled the Earth, where the legends of old are told anew, of the great battle in the last century where the loggers beat the bikers in a bare-knuckle brawl on main street and tossed their Harleys off the Calawah Bridge. That would require a hydraulic permit these days. This leaves some of us wondering, what are we supposed to do on a weekend without a festival?

The Forks Fudge Festival was a financial failure. The Hoh River

Lavender Festival had the potential to be larger than all these other festivals put together, but it wasn't.

As mayor of Oil City, I had to come up with a festival that would be better than all those other festivals put together. It would be a festival that would awaken a long-lost sense of civic pride.

Washington, D.C., may have its cherry blossoms. Portland may have roses, but Oil City has skunk cabbage! These beautiful and historically significant flowers showcase the beauty of our fair city to the world and beyond.

Oil City at the mouth of the Hoh River was named for the rich oil deposits that were sure to be found by the canny investor. The oil was first discovered by the local bears, who used to wallow in the stuff to keep their coats shiny. Native Americans who tried this were said to have died shortly afterwards. The effects on the bears remain unknown. The locals dug out the bear wallows and lined them with spruce limbs, and the oil rush was on.

Oil City, once called "The Pearl of the Hoh," had fallen on hard times when I became mayor. The citizens were revolting. They said I bought the election with fish but all the evidence was barbecued. My job as mayor was to revive to town and give its' citizens a sense of civic pride that had been missing for too long.

That's why I developed the "Stumps of Mystery" destination theme resort. Like the skunk cabbage, stumps have always been an important part of our heritage. Each stump is as unique as a snowflake. One stump alone is just a dead tree, but many stumps together form a clear-cut, or what we call a temporary meadow. The stumps do so much, giving us roads, hospitals and a system of education that's in the top 20th in the world! The "Stumps of Mystery" resort development would be the first in the country to feature the latest rage in wilderness survival: "Glam Stumps." These are not your grandpa's stumps. The Stumps of Mystery will feature carpeting, Naugahyde and hot and cold running stuff. Lodging tax and fumigation fees from the glam-stumps would fund many important cultural activities, such as the Skunk Cabbage Festival.

To the Native Americans, the skunk cabbage was known as a

starvation food. It kept people alive in the time before the salmon. That would have been after the glaciers had melted and before the first salmon colonized our rivers. When the first salmon arrived, the skunk cabbage was rewarded with an elk blanket, a war club and rich soil along the river where it is found to this day. The Skunk Cabbage Festival would have reminded everyone that once the salmon were gone, we would have to go back to eating skunk cabbage. There would be a wood-splitting contest right on Main Street as part of the interactive skunk cabbage parade and precision wood-stacking drill team demonstration event with cash and prizes for the first, largest and most artistic skunk cabbage.

All leading to the chili contest (with no goat or bear meat allowed) at the Oil City Center for the Performing and Culinary Arts. The theme of this year's extravaganza was, "Those who ignore history are doomed to eat skunk cabbage."

13

MEMORIAL DAY.

The Memorial Day weekend marks the traditional opener of tourist season on the Olympic Peninsula. Experts were predicting a big run of tourists, and I couldn't wait to go out and be a tourist with them. I had been working for weeks to get my boat ready for the big three-day weekend of fishing and camping. It's not easy to get a fishing boat outfitted properly. From the heated pole holder to the guide-model bottle opener, there are a lot of little details that can make quality time on the water. I thought I could get my boat all wired together in time for the big three-day weekend but something just wasn't right. The boat was missing a crucial part, a small American flag decal on the stern. Patriotism may be "the last refuge of a scoundrel," but it's better than no refuge at all. All I know for sure is that once I put that flag on the stern of my boat I started catching more and bigger fish. You can't argue with success. I'd rather have luck than skill. When it was time to repaint the boat to get ready for the big three-day weekend, I carefully peeled the little adhesive flag off and put it with some important papers for safekeeping. Then I lost the important papers.

I first put that American flag on my boat back in 2001. Our country had just been attacked by suicidal terrorists who killed thousands of people in one of the darkest days of our history. People were scared. They prayed to God for the safety and security of our country. People were putting American flags on everything. You could stop and buy an American flag at any gas station, grocery or hardware store in the country. I should have stocked up when I had the chance because just a few years later it became difficult to buy an American flag in America. I looked for weeks for an American flag for my boat without much luck. At first, I was discouraged then it became a challenge to buy an American flag in America. Maybe it's a good thing we are so apathetic. It must mean the war on terror is going well. The politicians haven't mentioned God lately. All we care about is a three-day weekend and the price of gas. Wasn't it just a few years ago, we were praying to God to save the United States? That might be foxhole religion but how soon we forget, it's better than no religion at all. God save The United States.

14

MEMORIAL DAY – THE STUPID TAX

It was almost daylight on the Quileute, a river formed by the confluence of the Sol Duc and Bogachiel. We were fishing. There was a dull roar coming from beyond the horizon which would indicate the surf was up. Salmon and steelhead like to come surf into the mouth of the river on the big waves. A rough sea helps the fish to dodge the sharks, seals and sea lions that congregate at the mouth of the river, but it's dangerous for boats. Just lucky we were on the river. It was calm with fog. We listened for the fish to roll, but there was another sound. It was the unmistakable whine of a Coast Guard helicopter. Coasties don't fly around in the dark and fog just for fun. We knew something bad had happened. I thought of all the people I have known who have gone down to the sea in ships and not come back. Many of them had no choice in the matter. They had to make a living. You don't catch fish unless you fish. Maybe they gambled on the weather and lost. Sometimes boats just sink for no apparent reason.

Sure enough, a later report said a fishing boat had sunk off La Push in the night. The skipper had gone down with the ship. The vessel and the captain haven't been found. As tragic as that was, it is not unusual out in what is known as the "Graveyard of the Pacific". After a while you just assume when you hear a helicopter something bad has happened.

The first time I saw La Push back in the early '70s there were two ambulances parked on main street with drowning victims who had wrecked down south by the Quileute Needles. The Quileute Bar can be deadly. This is dangerous water and not just for fishing boats. A Coast Guard life boat crew was lost here while attempting a rescue. A Coast Guard helicopter crashed in the power lines.

One day a kayaker showed up in La Push. He was paddling to Hawaii. After a couple of weeks, he washed up somewhere up on the coast of British Columbia. Then a guy paddled by in a kayak on his way to San Diego. Modern adventurers assume if they get into trouble it's just a matter of punching in a device and someone will come to the rescue. They hike up into the mountains in a blizzard assuming that if there is trouble they can just push another button and rangers will run to the rescue. These people like to float the rivers without walking them first, wreck their boat, push another button and expect search and rescue to show up just like on TV. The rescuers invariably have to risk their own lives to save others who have chosen to ignore the weather. That's stupid. If the government is short of money, instead of increasing license fees they should come up with a tax on being stupid. They'd balance the budget in no time.

15

MEMORIAL DAY – THE GREAT WHITE FLEET.

There are those who consider history a recurring process of decay. Evidence of this theory occurred on the Port Angeles City Pier last Saturday morning. A single Coast Guard cutter was the only vessel in attendance to celebrate the 100th anniversary of the 1908 visit of the Great White Fleet to Port Angeles. The Coast Guard has been saving lives here since the Cutter Snohomish was stationed here in 1910, but Port Angeles was a Navy town first. In 1895, Rear Admiral Beardslee brought the U.S. Navy Pacific Squadron to Port Angeles for the summer. Beardslee had just returned from Alaska where he had stopped the slave trade, freed native prisoners, named Glacier Bay and opened the Chilkoot trail. For the next forty-years the arrival of the Navy ships in Port Angeles heralded the start of the biggest party in Washington State. The Navy fired its big guns, launched torpedoes, staged night attacks and mock landings. The Navy's 10,000 sailors doubled the population of Port Angeles. What was a boring, isolated frontier town welcomed the Navy with open-arms.

The first Clallam County Fair was held in honor of Admiral Beardslee who spent so much time fishing at Lake Crescent they named a species of trout after him. The Naval Elks Lodge was built in 1913 with 10 senior Navy officers as charter members. There were parades, concerts, ship's tours, baseball games, picnics and more.

The local moon-shiners had to work overtime. An old timer told me the local girls would wear "wool socks in the spring, silk stockings in the fall."

Then in May of 1908, part of President Theodore Roosevelt's Great White Fleet anchored inside of Ediz Hook. The fleet had been sent on a world cruise looking for what the president called, "a feast, a frolic or a fight." It was part of Roosevelt's "Talk softly, carry a big stick" policy.

The Kaiser noticed this maneuver left our Atlantic seaboard undefended. He offered Roosevelt the use of the German navy in case we had a problem with Britain while our Navy was on the other side of the globe. The Germans called Roosevelt's "Big Stick" a "palm twig." The New York Times revealed some of the "armor" on the older battleships was made of wood and canvas. The Great White Fleet was a diplomatic phenomenon. It was met at every port with lavish entertainments and specially inflated prices.

The world cruise of the Great White Fleet was supposed to open the doors of trade with China. It was imagined that 400 million starving Chinese peasants would buy excess American agricultural and industrial products. Britain had used two Opium Wars to open trade doors with China. We hoped to wean the Chinese off British opium with American tobacco. It was all part of what Rudyard Kipling called "The White Man's Burden." President Roosevelt said it was "bad poetry but great, good sense." The British called it, "philanthrope plus 5%." It was imperialism with a moral purpose to Christianize. In 1900, Mark Twain called it "bedraggled, besmirched and dishonored."

The Great White Fleet visited Japan after a reluctant invitation. No wonder. The Japanese had their trade door forced open in 1853, when Commodore Perry fired a 13-gun salute in Tokyo Bay. The Japanese learned the strategic importance of a modern navy. The British helped them build one. The Japanese form of Imperialism, the so-called Co-Prosperity Sphere would start a war in the Pacific that consumed millions of human lives.

The Port Angeles centennial of the visit of the Great White Fleet last Saturday night was a subdued affair. There were no Navy ships. The cross-dressers had taken over the Naval Elks Lodge and Lake Crescent was only opened for catch and release fishing. Somewhere, Admiral Beardslee rolled over in his grave.

16

MEMORIAL DAY – THE FISH CAMP.

It's the simple things that I enjoy most about the fish camp, like the smell of burning driftwood and watching the sparks from the fire shoot up into the sky to join the stars before they fade. Or land on your tent to smolder as you remember you forgot the fire extinguisher. Then there are the night sounds of the wilderness. The distant hoot of the owl, the electric crackle of the bug zapper and the gentle murmur of a twenty-five hundred-watt gasoline-powered generator that tells you its summertime and the living is easy. Experienced campers know you must organize your supplies and prioritize your equipment to maximize your enjoyment of the outdoors. Life in the wilderness can test a woodsman's skill. There's a lot more to wilderness survival than being able to start a fire with just a single highway flare, cauterize a wound with gunpowder or siphon gas. The first rule of camping is to avoid taking along a lot of useless stuff that you just don't need.

Still it's the little things that can make a big difference between a memorable outdoor experience and a life-threatening disaster that tests the endurance of the human spirit. I once knew a camper who put all his food in plastic bags to cut down on weight and save space. Unfortunately, he was too busy to label the plastic bags, relying instead on a keen culinary instinct to tell the difference between sugar and spice. I carefully measured a cup of borax, a type of powdered soap used to cure fish eggs for bait, into the morning hotcake batter. Breakfast was served to the campers without a single complaint. They must have known. Camp cooks are chosen by a time-tested process where anyone who complains about the cooking is the new camp cook.

After breakfast, there were activities involving a foot race to the restroom facilities. I avoided the shame and disgust of the pit toilet with what could be the most important piece of camping equipment to come along since the turkey fryer: the camper's portable flush toilet. When using the camper's flush toilet, you really should read the instructions and maybe not enjoy the use of this product inside your tent. Especially while leaving an overfilled camper's espresso maker on top of your 60,000 BTU propane crab-cooker. After the fire I wished I remembered to pack the wet-dry camper's vac. Instead I shoveled out the tent the best I could and tried to dry the mess with a gas catalytic heater and a battery powered ceiling fan. That's when I noticed my queen-sized camper's air bed was as flat as a soapy pancake. I tried to find the leak by pumping the air bed up with my camper's air compressor, but the batteries were dead.

By then it was time for a relaxing morning shower. Whoever said fish and company smell after three days never went camping where it is possible to stink after a couple of hours. That's no problem with the propane-powered hot water heater and the adjustable jet nozzle shower head inside the collapsible camper's shower stall. Be sure to follow all safety instructions and check the temperature reading on your camper's shower system, or you could get scalded and go hopping around the campground like a singed grease monkey.

The rest of the day I spent doing the chores that need to get done to keep a fish camp running smoothly. I changed the oil in the generator and filled it with regular gas. I put white gas in the heater, replaced the batteries in the fan and compressor and refilled the propane cylinders on the turkey fryer, crab cooker, hot water heater and lanterns. By then it was time for dinner which was hotcakes again.

17

TOURIST SEASON – AN OLYMPIC PENINSULA DRIVING GUIDE

From the rugged acidified ocean seashore to the majestic shrinking glaciers the recreational wonderland we call the Olympic Peninsula has more diverse and delicate ecosystems than you can shake a stick at. Pack a lunch, grab a camera, cell phone, pepper spray, antacids, highway flares, rubber suit and barn boots, and don't forget your state park, national park, national forest, federal wildlife refuge and tribal permits and hit the road it's tourist season. Tourists come here from all over the world to clog up our roads. Some of them drive as bad as the locals.

You cannot be in a hurry here. It's just too frustrating to think you're going to get anywhere on time. When we have to stop and wait for a ferry or the Hood Canal Bridge to open for a Trident submarine you have to figure that's a small price to pay for the freedoms we enjoy. That submarine carries the equivalent of all of the explosives used in World War II. It's been said that a single Trident submarine represents the world's third largest military power. The skipper of that sub has an awesome responsibility for the lives of his crew, the security of this nation and the future of humanity. He probably doesn't care about a few carloads of tourists stuck on the bridge no matter how bad they need to use the restroom.

Of course, the tourist can always avoid the torture of being stuck on the Hood Canal Bridge on their journey to the Peninsula by taking the ferry from Whidbey Island to Port Townsend. It's a scenic cruise where the Strait of Juan de Fuca, the Georgia Strait, Hood Canal, Admiralty Inlet and Puget Sound converge in a tide-ripping cauldron of rolling waves and tide rips. Riding the Port Townsend ferry is like being on the Titanic with cell phones. If you should arrive in Port Townsend safely use caution. You may be asked to sign a petition.

You can still access the Olympic Peninsula and avoid the Port Townsend ferry with that other death wish, a drive around Hood Canal. Be prepared to be stuck in an endless line of crawling traffic on a road so crooked that it seems to be going in circles. The only thing tourists hate more than the twisted routes to get to the Olympic Peninsula is having to take time out of their white-knuckle road rally vacation to stop for highway construction.

"We had to wait twenty minutes!" a tourist sobbed. It was obviously too much to bear. They had to spend the whole time in a dead zone where the phones wouldn't work! How could they be expected to navigate the rest of their day from Lake Crescent to the Sol Duc, Cape Flattery, La Push and the Hoh Rainforest in time to make it to Ocean Shores for lunch? They had to catch a flight that night, and you know what a hassle that can be. Tourists want to get somewhere fast. To do that they need to pass other cars. The need to pass the car ahead of you, no matter how many cars are ahead of it, is one of man's most primal urges. This can be complicated by others employing the same maneuver from the opposite direction.

The Olympic Peninsula is an excellent place to view wildlife. Deer come to the roadways to feed on the lush native vegetation. No expense has been spared planting "deer-licous" stands of elderberry and current bushes mulched with beauty bark along sections of the highways, making it a great place to see deer. The deer have a very finely-honed sense of revenge left over from hunting season. They get even by jumping in front of cars at the last second causing horrible wrecks. That's the bad news. The good news is it is now legal in the state of Washington to salvage a road kill. After all these years the government finally got something right.

With any luck at all you'll make it to Sequim. That's the good news. The bad news is Sequim has an elk herd that blocks the highway whenever the animals feel like it. Once a quiet little dairy farming town, Sequim has turned into a retirement center we call God's Waiting Room. Keep moving. There are so many worse places to see. Deer Park is at the end of a single lane dirt road that will make you kiss the ground if you ever see pavement again. Also known as Deer Fly Park for the tremendous thirst of the insect population, this scenic area provides a majestic viewpoint to many more miles of bug-infested forest. There's a picnic area and a small campground. As I drove through I thought the friendly campers we're waving at me but they weren't. They were swatting at bugs. Activities at Deer Park include slapping each other as an excuse for swatting insects and trying to eat while keeping the bugs off your food. Remember to dress in many layers of clothing since the bugs are liable to eat their way through the first couple of them. Instead of going to Deer Park you might just make a donation to the local blood bank. I wouldn't send my worst enemy to Deer Park but a tourist? Heck yeah.

Inevitably the tourist reaches Port Angeles. It's a town that's seventeen miles from everywhere.

Seventeen miles to the north across the treacherous Strait of Juan de Fuca there is Victoria, British Columbia, Canada. They speak Canadian, eh? There is no Canadian word for "Sewage Treatment Plant." The City of Victoria's mascot is a little brown figure they call "Mr. Floatie". Victoria's city motto is "Flush twice it has to make it to Port Angeles."

It's also seventeen miles south of Port Angeles to scenic Hurricane Ridge within Olympic National Park. Visitors are asked to travel lightly. Drive across the traffic counter. Get an informative brochure printed on recycled paper and leave. That would be too easy.

For that special-someone you really don't like I would suggest a side trip to the nearby Badger Valley. Named for some imaginary badgers a pioneer thought he saw, Badger Valley is a lot like Deer Park except you have to hike into a hole to swat bugs. Then instead of driving away to escape the numberless tormentors you have to crawl out of an impossibly steep hornet infested valley. Keep an eye on the weather. The worst hiking tragedy to ever occur in Olympic National Park happened on the trail to Badger Valley. On September 30 1967, a father and a son died in a blizzard. Both of them had sleeping bags and extra clothes in their packs when their bodies were found in five-foot snow drifts a half a mile from the trail head. They don't call it Hurricane Ridge for nothing. It can be very dangerous country. Be aware that while you're hiking to Badger Valley the marmots are trashing your car.

Seventeen miles to the west of Port Angeles you will find Lake Crescent but there are so many worse places to see on the way like, the Elwha River. Where the unfortunate tourist can find themselves up the treacherous Whiskey Bend Road. While it is not true that the road was built by following the sheriff who was chasing a moonshiner through the woods it might as well have been. Inevitably the tourist comes to a trailhead. Leaving their vehicle at the mercy of the gangs of bandits who patrol our national parks and steal from the unsuspecting who leave valuables in their cars, our tourist begins walking to one of the more disappointing destinations in the Olympics: Goblin Gates.

Named by members of the 1889 Press Expedition who may have been suffering the effects of the Whiskey Bend Syndrome, Goblin Gates makes you wish our explorers would have kept the Indian name, whatever that may have been. I have stared at Goblin Gates for years and never seen a goblin. W.C. Fields, yes, but no goblins. Bitter and disillusioned, our tourist continues to the next practical tourist joke: Geyser Valley. Named by that same impressionable Press Expedition for an imaginary auditory phenomenon, Geyser Valley has no geysers. Years of searching by this wilderness gossip columnist has revealed no trace of geysers in this once pristine wilderness valley. A hike through the present-day Geyser Valley is about as scenic as walking through a gravel pit. The old growth forest of Geyser Valley, with its ancient trees and fluffy moss, was recently flushed down the river by a massive flood event, leaving a desolate wasteland that will take decades to heal. Even worse, since Geyser Valley is deep within the boundaries of Olympic National Park, a World Heritage Site,

Biosphere Reserve and crown jewel of the national park system, there are currently no loggers to blame for the incident.

Continuing up the Elwha trail, our tourist encounters the effects of the decayed infrastructure in our national parks. Frequent signs along the trail commonly post blatantly inaccurate mileage readings when I know for a geologic fact what with plate tectonics and all, the trails have gotten longer since I was hiking them as a kid. Inevitably our tourist reaches Humes Ranch. This once legendary fleshpot of the upper Elwha sits decayed and abandoned to remind the tourist they missed the party by a hundred years or so.

The Humes Ranch Cabin was built around 1900 by the Humes brothers who were on their way to the Klondike Gold Rush at the time, but they decided to settle in the Elwha Valley instead. The Humes brothers were varmint hunters who killed wolves, cougar and bear for the bounties that were paid at the time. They also guided parties of mountaineers and hunters deep into the interior of the Olympics. Grant Humes was a writer who in his later years said that there was more to hunting than killing animals. He established a game refuge on the ranch.

With the passing of the Humes brothers, the cabin was abandoned until 1940 when Herb Crisler moved in with his new bride Lois. The Crislers spent years filming what would become the Disney movie "Olympic Elk," using a Humes Ranch as a base of operations. The social scene at Humes Ranch is described in excruciating detail in the tell-all book "An Olympic Mountain Enchantment" by Ruby El Hult. She was a young journalist from Seattle when she came to Port Angeles in 1949 to write about the Olympic Peninsula in a book that would eventually be called "The Untamed Olympics." Ruby describes Humes Ranch as a busy place where as many as 50 people stopped for a visit one Memorial Day weekend. The Crislers were accommodating hosts who supplied their overnight guests with trout, fresh vegetables and hot rocks that were to be put in the sleeping bag to keep warm at night. Which inevitably lead to a complaint from a lonely male hiker,

"You mean with all of these pretty girls around I have to sleep with a rock?" The good news is that The Park Service restored this historic cabin. The bad news is that they took away the welcome mat. No camping is allowed. The unlucky tourist is advised to move along to encounter even more environmental degradation at Lake Crescent.

It's located in a haunted valley cursed by evil spirits since that fateful day in the dim past when the Quileute and the S'Klallam were having a battle. The evil giant Seatco stood upon Mount Storm King and buried the combatants under a rock-slide that separated Lake Crescent from Lake Sutherland. Ever since then there's been something weird about Lake Crescent. The natives avoided Lake Crescent and so do I. You don't need a fishing license to fish in Lake Crescent since it's in a national park. You will need an attorney to figure out the rules that all pretty much boil down to the same word: No.

The road around Lake Crescent follows an old elk trail. It's greasy and treacherous after a rain, and it rains all the time. Just across the lake you will find an even worse route. The Spruce Railroad Trail is the only place I have gotten a tick. Others have gotten them as well. Fortunately, there have been no cases of Lyme disease, but I ain't going to be the first one. There are even rumors of poison oak along this trail. Yuk!

West of Lake Crescent you are in logging country. You may see a road sign that says "Danger falling trees." Do not to be alarmed. Many loggers can hit a stake with a falling tree but darned few of them can hit a moving target. Where there are loggers, there are log trucks. Tourists frequently complain that log trucks act like they own the road. Do the math. A fully loaded log trucks weighs around 90,000 lbs. You don't. Log trucks act like they own the road because they do. You can't outdrive them. Pull over and let them by at every opportunity.

Forks was once the self-proclaimed logging capitol of the world. Then the loggers were blamed for endangering the spotted owl, the marbled murrelet and the bull trout in books and newspapers printed on paper made from wood the loggers cut. The survival of the loggers was threatened. They have become an endangered species whose population continues to decline.

South of Forks there is another great place to send tourists, the Hoh Oxbow Campground. Finding adequate restroom facilities in the wilderness could be one of the most important survival skills you can have. Our tourist visitors are unaccustomed to the local diet that relies heavily on the three basic food groups: grease, sugar and alcohol. Add the effects of sleep deprivation and mixed medications to the stress of a vacation grudge match with a vengeful significant other and the surely brood of teenage demon-spawn and it's no wonder you find yourself trapped in the outhouse of the doomed at the Hoh Oxbow campground. Most folks won't be able to stay inside longer than two seconds. Anyone who stays in longer than 30 seconds is presumed disabled from the fumes. A rescue attempt would be futile.

Not all wilderness adventurers however, are cut from the same cloth. There are some who are able to endure the rigors of the pit toilet for periods of a minute or more and emerge from the ordeal with no ill effects. Like the camper who was laying in his tent one night and heard a rustling sound that upon investigation, seemed to be coming from some sort of varmint beneath the tent floor. We have a saying in the deep dark woods that a man's best friend is a good sharp ax. It was not true in this case. Our camper grabbed an ax and chopped the tent floor to pieces to reveal the true identity of the nighttime visitor: the civet cat or spotted skunk.

It is an eternal wilderness truth that you can never find a flashlight when you need one. The tent zipper will stick when you least expect it. No matter, our screaming camper tore his way out of the tent to emerge gasping in a refreshing Hoh rainforest sprinkle. Unfortunately, the skunk was fatally injured. The soggy camper crawled back into the leaky tent in a vain effort to find his keys so he could start his truck and turn on the heater. Big drops of rain splattered like buckshot forming a bloody, skunky pool in the middle of the tent.

Dawn's early light found our camper swathed in a leaky down sleeping bag that had been chopped up in the mayhem. Unable to find the keys to his truck, he left a trail of feathers to the outhouse on his way to setting a record for staying in the longest. There I discovered the secret to enduring the outhouse of the doomed. Get sprayed by a skunk first, and a trip to the outhouse will seem like a day at the spa.

If the tourists survive the outhouse of the doomed, they are free to continue on to an even greater danger, the Pacific Ocean. People should stay away from the ocean. Our ocean beaches are a treacherous mix of deadly rip tides and surf logs that kill. Tourists are advised to keep moving south until they cross the Quinault River Bridge attaining the ultimate goal of the Olympic Peninsula tourist industry: getting them to leave.

18

TOURIST SEASON – BRAVE NEW TATTOO.

It's unfortunate that many of our tourist visitors are confused by the Washington State Discover Pass. It is just one of many passes, fees and permits that are required to get out of your car on the Olympic Peninsula. All these permits and the anxiety of having the right one at the right place negatively impact the quality of an American tradition: the family vacation. A recent visit by some tourist friends was a good example. They just wanted to go fishing. First, they stopped to get a fishing license with a stewardship access permit and a Discover Pass and a national park pass, just to be sure to be legal.

"What about a Forest Service pass?" I asked. As a fishing guide, I see myself as a goodwill ambassador for the tourist industry, a sort of a wilderness concierge who can allay the anxiety of modern travel restrictions through the maze of bureaucratic zones that our country has been divided into.

"I don't have a Forest Service pass." Dad sobbed. It was out of my hands now.

"Quick, get in the back of the truck!" I yelled, covering them with sacks of garbage and black plastic. I drove upriver and launched the boat. Dad and the kid emerged from the back of the truck a little worse for wear to the amusement of some other fishing guides. I told the tourists to crouch in the bottom of the boat and not move and

I would get them out of there. It was the quickest fishing trip they ever went on. We didn't catch anything but we didn't get arrested, which is the true test of a successful outing these days. The fact is all these permits are just too much hassle. It's time to do away with the Soviet style paper permits and allow our tourist industry to join the electronic age. A simple barcode for each person would make it easier for us to get all the licenses, permits, tags and punch-cards that are required. A barcode would allow our public safety officials a greater opportunity to enhance the stewardship of our natural resources while protecting us from the social costs that are borne by us all. Futurists have long envisioned an interactive skin-mounted barcode that would list an individual permit status along with other vital sign information which could be used in polygraph analysis, blood alcohol/drug screening and a host of other data-gathering opportunities.

Recent news articles have described a number of new personal electronic devices that can be swallowed, implanted or tattooed on a person. A Google-owned company has developed an "electronic skin tattoo" that would allow people to listen to music without headphones and talk more clearly on their smart phones in a room full of people talking on their smart phones. In addition, the electronic tattoo could include a galvanic skin response detector that would measure the way your skin conducts electricity. This would be helpful in determining if the person is nervous, which could be a good indication that they are engaged in telling falsehoods or other questionable activities.

Don't worry the electronic tattoo is not to be confused with the Mark of the Beast mentioned in the Book of Revelation, no way. The Mark of the Beast goes on your forehead or right hand. The electronic tattoo would go on your throat or on a trendy collar around your neck. Developers have proposed a tattoo that would vibrate when your phone rings. The possibilities for vibrating tattoos are endless.

It may sound silly to have our public officials and law enforcement agencies going around inspecting everyone's barcode. Hopefully they won't have to. Experts predict that the same drone aircraft that have been used so successfully in the War on Terror will soon be circling the skies of America. Drones combine computers, GPS and aviation into a cutting-edge management tool that can be used by the many different government agencies that monitor our safety and administer our natural resources.

During a survey of the Olympic Coast Marine Sanctuary, a drone was able to swoop in and spy on colonies of sea birds and seals. These sea creatures had nothing to fear from the mechanical bird circling above them. Why should we? The small aircraft was characterized as not having to eat, sleep or have a mind of its own, which basically describes the ideal government employee. Almost every day brings a new use for these amazing machines.

Scientists have used drones to track sediment from the world-famous Elwha River dam removal project. While many more studies will have to be done, preliminary results indicate the stuff is going downstream. All across our nation these vigilant machines are being used by scientists to keep track of the pygmy rabbits in Idaho, mule deer in Nevada and sage grouse in Wyoming.

Scientists are not the only ones who benefit from these technological wonders. Farmers use drones to monitor crops. Engineers are using drones to watch our highways crumble. Drones have also been used in law enforcement to catch bad guys. Why not use drones to effectively manage our outdoor recreational activities?

While we cannot confirm or deny that these drones will be able to monitor and manage thousands if not millions of barcodes from a central planning location, imagine a world where you can never be lost, where your family and loved ones could be constantly protected by government oversight. With the miracle of the drone monitored personal interactive electronic devices, the authorities would know when you are sleeping and know when you're awake. They'd know if you are bad or good, so we'd be good for goodness sake. You'll have nothing to fear if you have nothing to hide.

Sure, some silly civil libertarians will whine about the Constitution, but what else is new? Should we have interactive barcodes for people? We'll thank ourselves later if we do the right thing now.

19

FATHER'S DAY – THE BROWN HAT SOCIETY.

By now we are all familiar with the Red Hat Society. It's a disorganization of women founded years ago by a woman who upon turning 50, decided to fulfill her dreams of self-fulfillment by walking around town with a red hat on. At first the goal was to get together to express individuality, celebrate sisterhood and do lunch. It didn't take long for things to spin wildly out of control. Now they get together for Caribbean cruises and national conventions. They get in touch with their inner little girl and honor the change that comes with age through a process of intense retail therapy. There is a Red Hat catalogue with everything from feather boas to underwear. All of which made me wonder: Why isn't there a similar organization for men? There must be a reason, something beyond the fact that men over 50 are too ornery and broke to get together for lunch. Maybe it's an identity crisis brought on by the changing role of men throughout history that has many men wondering just where we went wrong.

I suspect the trouble all started when man began to abandon the hunter-gatherer lifestyle, some 6,000 years before the present. Cities sprang up out of nowhere. Even back then every city had a dump. They are called middens. Archaeological excavations of middens offer a glimpse into the food, clothing and spiritual beliefs of lost civilizations. The evidence suggests that in prehistoric times it was the prehistoric men who took out the garbage. It may have been this division of labor that led to great leaps in human evolution. When early man went to the garbage dump he probably found something he couldn't believe someone else had thrown away. So, he took it back to his Stone-Age workshop and invented stuff ... the wheel, the pyramid and the back-scratcher. These labor-saving devices led to the technological advances that gave men a sense of their own self-worth.

It's a historical fact that throughout history and around the world behind every good woman there was a crew of men doing the heavy lifting. It was their hard work and dedication that made our country what it is today. In modern times, old men have become the one segment of our population that it's politically correct to ridicule. Watch how men are portrayed on TV. They're the ones who can't figure out how to change a roll of toilet paper.

Maybe men need something like the Red Hat Society to fulfill our dreams of self-fulfillment. We'll call it the Brown Hat Society. We'll celebrate our maleness the best way we know how, with obscure collections and unfinished projects we always meant to get back to. We'll get together to discuss our medical problems. If a man wears a brown hat in the woods, does that mean he's wrong? Of course, many men are completely colorblind. The brown hat could be green or red, we just don't care. The Brown Hat Society celebrates this diversity with a catalogue jammed full of everything from back-scratchers to underwear. As Brown Hatters, we'll celebrate the change in life that comes with advancing years. It would be a testimonial to when I had a dream, to turn 50 and walk the streets with a brown hat knowing it may be the only thing I have left. Until then, "Happy Father's Day".

20

THE FORKS FUDGE FESTIVAL.

The Forks Fudge Festival celebrates the fascinating history of fudge in this country. Our pioneer forefathers had to battle their way across deserts, plains and mountains before they could get here. Many did not make it. The Donner party was trapped for the winter in the mountains. We all know the story of how these unfortunate pioneer forefathers were reduced to cannibalism. Do you know why? The Donner Party had no fudge. There is a lot of history that you'll never read in a history book.

The Forks Fudge Festival will celebrate the importance of fudge and how it made our country what it is today. Unfortunately, founding the Forks Fudge Festival involves funding. I'm not going to beat around the bush. There are expenses with any worthwhile cause. With your cash or in-kind real estate donation you'll receive a free collectible "Forks Fudge Festival" bumper sticker. In addition, you'll want to fill out your application today for the Forks Fudge Festival credit card. Even if you've been turned down for a credit card before, even if you are legally dead, you cannot be turned down for the Forks Fudge Festival credit card. The Forks Fudge Festival credit card is good at any one of the hundreds of Forks Fudge Festival vendors.

Follow your nose to the French-fried fudge fingers booth. Purchase a unique, one-of-a-kind chainsaw sculpture made entirely of fudge. Do not pay for one full year for any fudge furniture. What's a festival without entertainment? You'll want to start starving yourself right now for the fudge-eating contest. Don't forget your splatter shield. I can't wait for the fudge toss. It could become an Olympic event. Young and old of all ages will thrill to the spectacle of hot-fudge wrestling. What's a fudge festival without royalty? Folks will be lining the streets to be named the next Forks Fudge Fairy. I foresee a fabulous future in the Forks Fudge Festival if we facilitate federal funding for fledgling family fudge factory franchises. Whip it and they will come. Using only the purest ingredients unless we can't, we can transform Forks into the fudge capitol of the world. I will be leading a series of fudge factory tours as soon as someone donates a bus. The tourists will flock in so thick we'll have to beat them off with a club. Let them eat fudge! See you at the Forks Fudge Festival!

21

JUNE 21 – THE LONGEST DAY.

It is the longest day and there is much to see between dawn and dusk. It begins with a thick blanket of fog that drips from the leaves of the alder trees like a light rain. There is a splash in the river. A swirl the size of a picnic table spreads across the surface of the still water where the salmon has jumped. Why do salmon jump? That has been a question of the ages. There are a number of theories. Some say the salmon jump to rid themselves of sea lice, a small parasite that stick to the fish in salt water but the sea lice will fall off the fish in freshwater anyway. Others say the salmon jump to loosen the eggs that they carry but it's common to see spawned-out salmon jumping in the river when they have no eggs. Others say salmon jump to orient themselves to landforms and navigate their way back to the precise area that they were spawned. This does not explain why spawned-out salmon jump. They die after spawning, so they are not going anywhere. Salmon generally jump when there are a lot of them around. This could mean salmon jump when they are happy. Despite all these opinions there's only one sure-fire way to know why salmon jumps and that is if it's on the end of your line. It is possible there is nothing more frustrating than to have salmon jumping all around you and not one of them will bite. That's when you know the fishing trip has turned into an adventure in bird watching.

Witnessing the attack of two bald eagles on a great blue heron must be one of the queasiest sights in nature. In the air the great blue herons glide in a slow lumbering flight that seems to take forever to get them anywhere. With their necks majestically folded and their legs hanging back like a rudder, they appear easy prey for an eagle. The only thing the herons have going for them is their exceptional wariness and a long sharp beak that looks like it could poke through a sheet of plywood. Eagles dive with long sharp talons and a beak meant for tearing flesh. You wouldn't think a great blue heron would have a chance against an eagle.

All at once out of nowhere the drama starts above us. Two eagles converge on a lone heron. Maybe the heron is trying to decoy the eagles away from a nest but it looks like the decoy is going to get eaten. Eagles catch geese, ducks and pelicans so you'd think a slow-flying heron wouldn't stand a chance. The lone heron appears doomed with two eagles closing in fast. There is nowhere for the heron to hide in the wide-open sky. The heron flaps its' wings spiraling higher in tight little circles denying the eagles their main tactic, a diving attack from above. The eagles pump their wings for all they're worth but fail to climb as fast the heron. The heron and the eagles climb higher and higher until they are just specks in the sky. The eagles tire and set their wings gliding off to easier prey. The heron glides away in the opposite direction. We sit in the boat realizing that not even the bird watching is working out this morning.

As the day unravels things can only get worse. This is confirmed when you realize that you are watching fish ducks. The mother merganser is feeding her tiny hatchlings a diet of baby salmon that just popped out of the gravel. The all-time record of baby mergansers in one hatch stands at 32! These saw-billed, fish-eating machines are a key indicator of the health of the river. When those worthless fish ducks disappear, the fishermen won't be far behind them. We see other hen mergansers are flying downriver to the ocean when they should be swimming with their chicks. If their chicks haven't hatched by now they aren't going to. This would indicate a dismal merganser nesting season with grave but as yet to be determined consequences for humans. While extracting specific data about the health of the planet by observing baby fish ducks or the lack of them can be problematic, it's safe to say that humans as a species are doomed.

Until then we are content to watch the birds. Bird watching is almost a blood sport when it is done right. Watching eagles hunt the baby ducks is one of the greatest thrills of nature unless it is an eagle engaged in hunting baby otters. The eagles are not particular this time of year. Their own hatchlings are back at the nest squawking for food from dawn until dark so the parents are liable to tackle anything.

The fog clears for the snow-capped Olympics to bask in the hot sun, a winters worth of snow melts all at once in every direction. You can hear the creeks in the mountains roaring down into rivers in the canyons making a chocolate milkshake of glacial till. You want to be careful on the river when the water is high. The current is fast and deep. The gray water hides gray rocks that lurk just below the surface. We float downriver until we see an attractive female on the beach. She appears unaware of our presence. Lithe as a thoroughbred with her cinnamon hair shining in the sun, she is a pretty thing. Since we are anchored up, I throw out a couple of plugs while my fishing friend ogles the elk with binoculars. Just then two spindly calves trot out onto the waters edge. The mother wades out into the river like she is going to cross. The river looks like a giant washing machine with enough logs stuck in to make deadly for anything without gills. The youngsters just stand there looking at mom so she wades back to shore and wallops their butts into the river.

A coyote trots out of the brush. It looks wet like it's been in the river. Coyotes hunt in packs. They must have been hunting these elk calves for a while. Now the calves are trapped on a gravel bar with the rapids on one side and a pack of coyotes on the other. The mother elk pushes the babies into the river then turns and charges back into the brush like she is going to stomp some coyotes. The baby elk disappear downstream swept away by the force of the current.

Hours later we float by one of the calves where it had washed up on a gravel bar. A pair of eagles is circling closer. The sun sinks behind an approaching fog bank. The mist returns to the valley. A salmon jumps into the twilight. It's the end of the longest day.

22

FOURTH OF JULY BEAVER.

Summer must be my favorite time of year to fish. The rivers are clearing after the spring runoff and the fishing can be terrific. On any given day, you can catch summer steelhead, spring Chinook and sea-run cutthroat. The fish seem to bite better when there are a couple of feet of visibility in the water. In fact, water clarity can determine fishing success. The fish can't bite what they can't see.

Maybe that's why it was so disturbing to observe on a Fourth of July float trip a brown-looking side stream spewing mud into the emerald blue river water. I wondered what sort of environmental criminal in this enlightened age of strict environmental regulations would dirty up a stream. I walked up the creek to find out. What I saw was enough to shock any environmentalist. Trees were cut right to the water's edge. An ugly pile of mud-plastered branches choked off the creek so tight not even a bull trout could wiggle through. What had once been a pristine stream in the wilderness had been turned into a stagnant pond of scummy water in the middle of a clear-cut. There were more piles of logging slash scattered across the pond.

You could tell that whoever had cut the trees was a real greenhorn. The high, ragged stumps gave that away. Some of the trees had been cut and left laying where they fell. I wondered what sort of sick animal would cut a tree down for fun.

"Beavers," my friend said. Mystery solved. The Fourth of July is a good time to appreciate the beaver. They personally financed the exploration and settlement of America with their own coats. The Hudson's Bay Company was formed in England in 1670. It's stated purpose was to find the Northwest Passage across the New World and thus a shorter trade route to the Orient. Along the way, they trapped beavers to finance their noble cause. The HBC eventually claimed a 670,000-square-mile domain in what we call the "Pacific Northwest" based upon the explorations of their fur brigades.

The United States claimed much of the same land based upon Captain Robert Gray trading 300 beaver furs to China after he found the Columbia River in 1792. Eventually the competing fur companies tried to kill every fur-bearer in a large area, to discourage anyone else from bothering to enter. For a while it seemed as if whoever skinned the most beavers could claim the most land.

Trappers were often the first Europeans the Native Americans encountered. The trappers were seen as a civilizing influence. They introduced gunpowder, metal and liquor to a Stone-Age culture. When the beaver were trapped out silk replaced the felt made from beaver fur in the fashion industry. The fur trade collapsed. The HBC moved north of the Canadian border. The United States took over what is now Oregon, Idaho, and Washington.

Now the beavers are worth more to the environment than they ever were as hats. The beavers work for free in making critical salmon habitat. A beaver pond is a refuge for baby fish in winter floods and summer's low water. The Fourth of July is a good time to thank the beavers for all they've done for our country.

23

FOURTH OF JULY – THE DECLARATION OF INDEPUNDITS.

Happy Fourth of July! I can think of no better time than the Fourth of July to celebrate the Declaration of Independence. It's hard to imagine the courage it took for the fathers of our country to sign this document. Any one of them could have been hung for treason against the British crown, King George III. Also known as "The Mad King," King George III was a lunatic. His tyrannical rule of the colonies was characterized by the American revolutionaries as "taxation without representation." It was a form of imperialism where people were taxed to support a government that did nothing for them but repress what the colonists considered their natural, legal and inalienable rights as human beings.

The right to life, liberty and the pursuit of happiness as stated in our Declaration of Independence has since been used as a blueprint by freedom-loving people around the world and throughout history to cast off the shackles of government tyranny.

A reading of the Declaration of Independence has been an essential element of America's birthday since it was first celebrated in 1777. However, since the United States Supreme Court decision that corporations are citizens, I think it may be way past time to amend and modernize the Declaration of Independence. It's time for all Americans to embrace the concept that corporations are just like us, only bigger. That does not mean corporations don't have feelings too. For too long corporations were denied the basic rights that were guaranteed to the rest of us consumers. While the court decision goes a long way to redress this historic wrong, we could do more. So here goes. The Declaration of Indepundits:

When in the course of corporate events it becomes necessary for one company to dissolve the business relationship with another and assume among the powers of finance, the separate and equal station to which the Federal Trade Commission and the Stock Market entitle them, a decent respect to the profits of corporations requires that they should declare the causes which impel them to liquidate their domestic assets.

We hold these truths to be self-evident, that all corporations are created equal, that they are endowed by consumers with certain unalienable rights that among them are executive pay raises, freedom from anti-trust regulations and the pursuit of profit. That to pursue these profits corporations are instituted among companies, deriving their just powers from the consent of the shareholders for the common good of us all. That whenever any form of Government becomes destructive of corporate profits, it is the Right of the Corporations to alter or purchase a new Government that should seem most likely to affect the safety and happiness of the corporations, their shareholders and consumers.

Prudence, indeed, will dictate that Governments long established should not be purchased for light and transient causes. But when a long train of abuses to corporate profits lowers their stock price, it is their corporate duty to lay off such a Government and purchase a new one, to provide new guards for their future corporate security.

We, therefore, the Corporations of the United States of America, appealing to the Supreme Judge of World Trade for the rectitude of our profits, do, in the name of our shareholders have the full power to levy war, conclude peace, contract alliances, establish commerce, purchase elections and do all other things which the military/ industrial complex does all of the time. With a firm reliance on government providence, we mutually pledge to each other our tax shelters, stock options and sacred profits.

24

THE SEQUIM LAVENDER FESTIVAL – LAVENDER TOUR OF THE DOOMED.

It's time once again for Sequim's annual Lavender Festival. It's only now that the statute of limitations thing wore off that I am free to write about my own humiliating experiences as a lavender farmer. It was a lavender-scented nightmare of treachery, greed and deceit amidst a post-agricultural landscape of retirement homes, box stores and strip malls we like to call Sequim. It's where a small but determined group of lavender farmers tried to keep one small section of our farming heritage unpaved for future generations to enjoy while creating the biggest traffic jam to ever hit the Olympic Peninsula. Where thousands of lost tourists circle endlessly in a lavender-induced fog competing for parking spaces with the locals.

I made a lot of mistakes when I first started out as a lavender farmer. I never should have said I was a lavender farmer. I only had one plant. It was a very old lavender plant but that did not give me an excuse to say I had the oldest lavender farm in the Sequim-Dungeness Valley. I was a journalist on assignment trying to do my duty to strip the dirty linen from the seamy underbelly of the lavender growing cabal.

Lavender is a short little plant you have to bend over to plant, weed or pick. All those pictures of smiling lavender farmers had one thing in common: They are not smiling. That is the unmistakable grimace of lower back pain from bending over to pick lavender. I'll never forget the year I threw my back out picking the very first lavender blossom of the season. It was just my luck it happened right before the Lavender Festival. I had a lot of chores to finish on my lavender farm before the lavender tour began. I was going to go to the dump. When the buzzards start landing in your driveway you know it's time. I was going to turn my fleet of wrecked boats into attractively elegant lavender planters. At the last-minute things started to go terribly wrong. My lavender recipe cookbook which included hundreds of trendy lavender dishes from lavender clam dip to lavender caviar finally came back from the publisher. It was printed in Esperanto.

Then tragedy struck. My lavender farm, the oldest lavender farm in the Sequim-Dungeness Valley was plowed into the swamp by a passing elk herd just before the lavender-worshiping hordes were about to descend. What could I do? What would you do? I went to the hardware store and bought every blue plastic tarp I could find and beat it back to the farm. I ran around covering woodpiles, wrecked boats and weed-choked ground with perky blue plastic tarps hoping it might all look like a field of lavender from a distance to the farm visitors, after the refreshments hit. I thought a couple of shots of lavender moonshine would grease the skids on any lavender farm tour. Little suspecting a nosey pack of revenuers would find my lavender distillery out in the woods and cut it up for scrap, sabotaging my celebration of all things lavender.

25

GRANDPARENTS DAY – FISHING WITH GRANDMA.

When I was a child a magical thing would happen every summer: Grandma would come for a visit. I had a fishing Grandma. When she retired to go fishing the trout population took a severe hit. She had a flame-red Valiant with a big V-8 and a push-button automatic transmission. It had a trunk big enough to hold enough supplies for an expedition. It could take several people to help unload the fiesta cake, 24-hour salad, cookies, oranges, grapes and more from the vast trunk.

Grandma's motto was, "You should never give up an opportunity for an outing or a trip." She believed, among other things that cherries should be canned with the pits taken out. Embroidering pillow slips and quilting on Tuesdays keeps your fingers nimble. The cookie jar should always be full and it is perfectly acceptable for growing boys to eat a whole pie. Her banana crème pie was a monument to the culinary arts. She did not skimp on the butter.

I could hardly wait for Grandma to show up for her yearly clamming and fishing trip. When fishing with her you didn't go around looking for pop bottles to turn in for money for treats, no. Grandma Neal not only had the classiest ride in the county she had plenty of cash to go with it. We'd hit the road for the beach at low tide and dig a washtub of clams then go out for burgers in a little shack right on the beach.

Once Grandma got her fill of clams we'd go fishing in the Elwha, a legendary trout stream in its day. We'd drive up the Olympic Hot Springs road and fish the holes along the road. There is some fast water in that stretch. I was fishing downstream from Grandma when she tumbled into the river. I tried to help as she went bobbing by but just then I hooked a 12-inch rainbow on a Herter's spinner. Grandma made it out okay though. After that Grandma Neal dropped us off along the river while she took a rest. We'd come back to the Valiant for lunch. A Grandma Neal shore lunch was a banquet fit for a king. After lunch Grandma would take a nap. We'd fish until we ran out of worms, head back to the Valiant and then drive back home for a fish fry.

Back at school I bragged I about my fishing Grandma. A classmate said Grandma didn't fish, she just sat in the car but he didn't understand. Grandma didn't have to fish. She could park that Valiant along any trout stream in the Western United States, turn her grandkids loose and go home with a basket of trout. That's a fishing Grandma in my book.

The good old days were too good to last. I turned into a worthless teenager tumbling down the slippery slope to the dark side. I started fly-fishing. Before long I was too busy to go fishing with Grandma Neal. She started going to Reno. She said it had a beautiful cathedral and playing cards kept your mind sharp. She had always believed in supporting the local bingo games. It might have affected her health. She only lived to be 100. When she died, we just figured the Good Lord needed a fishing Grandma more than we did.

26

GROUSE SEASON.

September might mean the end of summer but it signals the beginning of grouse season. Hunting season already started for bear hunters but I don't hunt bears. Once upon a time I shot a bear. It was an accident. I was cleaning my gun and it went off and tragically hit a bear. We held a celebration of life barbecue for the bear but the meat was tougher than grandma's Army boot. It seemed to grow while you chewed it. The bear hide was in prime shape though, until it got shot. Then it had more holes in it than one of my fish stories. I tried to tan the bear hide with the Indian cure, using a mash of brains, urine and liver but tanning a hide is a lot like writing a newspaper column. I ran out of brains at the end. Still, I thought a bear hide would make a nice throw rug for Ma, until she complained about the grease stains on the floor and how it set off her allergies.

I decided to stick to grouse hunting after that. Grouse is one of the finest-flavored birds there is. There are many fine recipes for grouse but they all call for the same thing: a grouse. I used to think the best way to hunt grouse was on horseback but I was just a kid and didn't know any better. I had a hunting horse. I trained the horse myself to do whatever he wanted. Like any two-year-old, that horse wanted to run. You had to get on him first. The horse was not crazy about the idea of running with somebody on his back. About the time you got one foot in the stirrup he would begin spinning and hopping while trying to bite and kick. Once you got on the hunting horse you had to hang on and keep low to the saddle to avoid overhanging limbs, which was tough to do while holding a rifle. We covered a lot of ground though. Every now and then a grouse would flush beneath the pounding hooves. That put the pedal to the metal as far as the colt was concerned. By the time you got him stopped we could be in the next county. Turning around to go back and look for the grouse meant we were heading back to the barn as far as the horse was concerned so there was almost no stopping him.

It was just your tough luck if he saw a coyote. That horse loved to chase coyotes. He loved to jump logs. If the coyote went under a log the horse would go over it. Once he even jumped over the hood of a Mustang convertible that was parked in the wrong place. I've often wondered what the two people in the back seat of the car must have been thinking when they parked there. Didn't they know it was grouse season?

27

LABOR DAY – THE 10 STAGES OF CAMPING GRIEF.

I really should have followed my own advice about camping on Labor Day weekend: "Don't."

Now it serves me right to suffer though the stages of camping grief. These include but are not limited to anticipation, denial, bargaining, depression, hopelessness, fear, bitterness and blame. The camping trip began with anticipation. Many species of wild life cue their migrations to a seasonal food source, so when the blackberries ripen on the Hoh River it's not unusual to see fishing guides congregate on a river bank for the expected pie or cobbler. When there was no blackberry cobbler I fell into a sense of denial where I thought we could get some cobbler if only it would stop raining long enough to pick some blackberries.

This lead to another stage of camping grief bargaining, where you hope things will get better if you move somewhere else but really who were we trying to kid? It's Labor Day. All of the campgrounds were full and you're stuck in a war zone where scary people want you to help them. They drove into the river and got stuck. This lead to another stage of the camping process: depression. In the old days, people traveled our rivers in canoes by poling them up the river. That is where you stood in the stern of the canoe and pushed it upstream with a pole. There is a story of an Indian chief that forbade the use of poles on the river near his village, insisting the people paddle their canoes for fear that the poles pushing down into the gravel would kill the salmon eggs in the spawning beds.

Fast forward to Labor Day weekend where people were joy-riding in the river until they got stuck. A truck represents many gallons of toxic waste in the river. This was an emergency but with all of the borrowed logging rigging we could find we could not move the wreck one inch. There was nothing we could do but watch the wreck leach chemicals into the river and lapse into another stage of camper's grief, hopelessness. This lead to a sense of fear as the campers cranked up a death-metal jam to eleven, began shooting semi-automatic weapons into the river and started a campfire that looked like a burning oil well. I heard something whistle like a bird call but all the birds had been scared away. That was the sound of bullets ricocheting. Must be why shooting on the river is not recommended, even if there is not a highway on the other side of the it. Bullets can ricochet off water in any direction.

The one of the great thing I have always liked about camping is how it brings people closer together. Unless you are huddled together behind an engine block hoping to dodge the hail flying lead. This can lead to still more stages of camper's grief engendering a sense of bitterness and blame on whoever wanted to go camping in the first place. Still, any camping trip you can walk away from is a good one.

28

THE BEAR CREEK CHILI CONTEST.

I'm not bitter about not winning the Bear Creek Chili Contest. I only entered it on the advice of my psychologist. He used to practice at a place called Parris Island. That sounded nice. We traded fishing trips for counseling sessions. He told me I was only as good as my next fish. I asked him if a chili contest would be the answer to all my problems. He said no but he needed someone to do the heavy lifting. Maybe I'm just too nice. I tried to help a friend. I didn't know you have no friends at a chili contest. Some people can be so competitive over the least little thing. The chili contest had become a chili war! It was time to break out the secret weapons: the bear sausage, the New Mexico green chilis and my mom. She had won a chili contest! I was sure she would be thrilled and delighted to pass the recipe on to the next generation of chili award winners.

For a while it looked like this chili contest was simply a matter of organizing my crew, mixing refreshments, and rehearsing my acceptance speech. Unfortunately, my entry in the chili contest was sabotaged from the very start. Mom claimed she forgot her chili recipe. When she dropped by to try my best effort, she said it was hot enough to "singe your gizzard." We were only allowed three hours to cook the chili and mine takes all day. Then my psychologist lodged a formal complaint with the chili judging committee. He claimed I had used a road-kill as an ingredient. It turns out burnt rubber is a banned substance! I left in disgrace.

Take it from me: It's never a good idea to leave your psychologist alone with your mother and a half-gallon of tequila. They were having such a good laugh I didn't want to interrupt. I sulked through the rest of the chili contest dodging packs of feral children riding bicycles with no body armor. Others were looking for coins hidden in a big pile of hay. There was a so-called pillow fight where children used gunny sacks full of hay to pummel each other. Still other children were engaged in a barbaric practice of swinging a rope around in circles which another unfortunate child was forced to jump over. All of which was conducted with no adult supervision, safety gear or warning labels.

That's when I noticed something very strange was going on here. Not one of these unfortunate children had a cell phone or a video game. Disturbingly, they had been left alone to amuse themselves outdoors without the safety net of electronic devices that any responsible parent would normally provide. I wondered how, in the richest country in the world could we as a society allow this to happen? Children are our greatest national resource. They should not be forced to jump to dodge threatening ropes, bully others with hay sacks or scrounge through an unsanitary pile of barnyard debris looking for coins to better themselves, no. The event organizers really should have hidden debit cards in the hay. The Bear Creek Chili Contest began as a charity event. Charity begins at home. Somebody needs to get these country kids a data plan.

29

THE FIRST DAY OF SCHOOL – CONFESSIONS OF AN ALTER BOY.

Like many in my class of Catholic school children in the '60s, I was convinced I was going to hell. That was the bad news. The good news was that all my friends would be there. A lot of my friends were altar boys and so was I. These days it is very popular to joke about and make fun of altar boys but in the old days of the Latin Mass you had to have your act together to be an altar boy.

Those unfamiliar with the Catholic faith probably don't know what a big job that was. After you learned Latin you were in charge of the water, wine, bread, candles, incense, bells, a medieval wardrobe and in some cases crowd control in everything from baptisms to funerals. Meanwhile there was no slouching, fidgeting or worse, sleeping, allowed. And that wasn't the worst thing you could do as an altar boy. The worst thing would be dropping the bread, which represents the body of Christ. Go dropping Jesus during communion and you'd find yourself serving six a.m. Mass with the new guys for the rest of your altar boy career. Screw-ups who couldn't light the candles, fire up the incense or pour water were never going to fast-track their way up to the big time, the holiday High Masses. That's where you made the big bucks. You could make up to five dollars for a midnight Mass, double shift with another High Mass the next day and make what was some pretty good dough in those days.

Then there was that other special perk that few realized: Being an altar boy meant you could skip a lot of school on religious grounds. People died all the time so there were funerals during the week. We called it the graveyard shift. I would have skipped school to go frog hunting at the time if I could get away with it, but serving Mass at funerals was the only alibi that would pass the parental guidance committee. It didn't take long for the money and the free pass out of class to go right to our heads. We thought we were better than everyone. We could look down our nose at the drunks who only came to church once a year at midnight on Christmas Eve or Easter, while we went almost every day. Never mind we were sneaking the sacramental wine. What the heck, we smoked and chewed so pounding a little vino first thing in the morning was no big deal.

Still, being an altar boy was not without its special challenges and humbling episodes that confirmed our worst suspicions: We were as rotten as anyone else. People talk about seven deadly sins but they never mention the one that might have been worse than all the others put together to an altar boy: flatulence. You had only one chance to get away with it. You wanted to be ringing the bells during the attack and maybe move along and light off a big lump of incense really quick before the guilty party could be identified. I often think of this when people refer to Catholic Mass as "bells and smells".

Eventually I started going to a bigger church. It contained one of the Earth's greatest treasures: silence. This church was so big it had mountains, giant trees and a river running through it. I took my priest friend out to my church on the Queets River and confessed I was a poor excuse for an altar boy. He caught a nice Coho and all my sins were forgiven.

30

HISTORY DAY – THE DUNGENESS HISTORY PROJECT.

February was always a favorite month to fish. It's when we caught the biggest steelhead of the year. The old guy that showed me how to catch steelhead didn't own a tackle box. He carried a wicker creel. Inside he had a few leaders tied up with some split shot and a jar of eggs cured in sugar and salt. Once in a while Harry would get fancy.

"We started tying red yarn on our leaders after the War," he said. That would be the big one, WWII. The rest of Harrys' gear looked like it had been through the war. The guides on his rod and his reel were held on with electrical tape. He would strip some line off an old fly reel and swing his little glob of home-cured caviar out into the river, usually less than ten feet from shore. One morning he caught both our limits before I untangled the bird's nest of fouled line in my fancy modern gear.

"You have to feel the bite," Harry said as I packed the fish to the truck. That hurt. A fishermen's ego can be as delicate as the most fragile eco-system. I tried to console myself with the fact that Harry had a 50-year head start on me fishing steelhead. I was just a new guy with a lot to learn but I thought it would be nice if he let me catch a fish once in a while.

My hurt feelings didn't keep me from showing up at his house bright and early the next morning. That was stupid. Harry never caught a steelhead before ten and he wasn't about to be rushed. We were going to have breakfast. That was very fortunate. Harry and his wife Lena were great cooks. They did all their cooking on a wood cook stove which was prone to chimney fires once it got hot enough to boil water. Harry claimed there was nothing like a chimney fire to take the chill off in the morning but he worried about igniting a deposit of bat guano that was up in the attic. He meant to shovel the bat guano out before it caught on fire since it was the best garden fertilizer you could get, next to spawned out salmon.

Along with the bats Harry and Lena kept a variety of other remarkable pets. They had a dog who could tell them who came by the house for a visit when they were gone. There was a chicken that laid her eggs on the back porch, a family of skunks that loved ice cream, pack rats, civet cats and mice that infested their hundred-year old house that Harry claimed was built by a pair of Norwegian bachelors who never once used a square, tape measure or a level. The bathroom was the draftiest room in the house so it served as a cold storage in winter. Harry kept the steelhead in the bathtub until it was time to put them in the smokehouse. Lena wondered just when he was going to get those fish out of the tub so she could take a bath but Harry wasn't going to run the smokehouse for just four fish. We were going to catch some more. That was the old days when you could depend on the Dungeness River for a food supply. Harry gave me one of the best recipes for cooking fish. Build a fire of alder wood. Strip a chunk of green alder bark from a tree. Place the fish on the bark and the bark upon the coals. Cook slowly until the bones pull loose. This could take a while.

I could hardly wait for Harry's smoked fish but we had to catch some more. It was a perfect day for fishing, what we call "steelhead weather" about thirty-three degrees and raining. Driving upriver, I thought the rain might turn to snow. That was a concern because Harry was not too sure on his feet. I was worried enough about getting him to the river when he said.

"I think I'm having a stroke," I panicked, jammed on the brakes turned the truck around.

"Where're we going? He asked.

"The hospital!" I said. Harry said not to worry,

"It won't hit until tomorrow. Let's go fishing." I stopped the truck and looked at Harry. He appeared perfectly normal, calm and relaxed, serene even. Harry told me to go back up the river. He said it wouldn't really hit for a day or two because that's the way it was with his other stroke.

I didn't know about the other stroke. I knew about his heart attack. That started when we were road hunting that fall with his friend Boone.

Harry must have been in his '70's. Boone was 80 something. I had a government job locating historic sites, structures and artifacts on the Olympic Peninsula and nominating them to the National Register of Historic Places. This was the 1970's. The competition was stiff. Other National Register properties being discovered at the time included the Manis Mastodon Site near Sequim where a 14,000, year old spear point was found in a mastodon rib. This represented the oldest human activity in the Pacific Northwest. At Ozette they were excavating what came to be known as the American Pompeii where a village was buried by a mudslide preserving enough artifacts to fill the museum at Neah Bay. Things were not going so well on my research project. The most historic things I had found so far was a three-hole outhouse, some topless statuary at a Eugenics lab and the largest known hot-cake griddle in the Olympic Mountains. I was getting desperate. I needed to discover something cool so I could keep my government job.

The history of the Olympic Peninsula from its' official discovery by the Spanish Captains Heceta and Quadra in 1775 to the coming of the railroad in 1913 occurred in less than 150 years. To put this in perspective there is over 300 years between these historic benchmarks on the east coast of the United States. The Olympic Peninsula's relatively short history of European occupation meant that in the 1970's there were still people alive who may have listened to their great grand-parent's description of the arrival of the white man, what the Native Americans called "the floating house people." There were others who had grown up on the remote homesteads that their parents had chopped out of the wilderness. They survived on what they could gather from the land, out of the river or from the ocean. They logged, trapped and bounty hunted varmints. They followed elk trails until the trails became roads. It was a pattern of settlement that had leap-frogged across the continent until it reached the end of the last frontier, the Pacific Ocean.

By the time I got there the abandoned remains of the last frontier were sinking into the underbrush. Documenting the scattered debris of what was left was like taking a census of a wasteland. It was a journey back in time guided by some fast disappearing old-timers. I drove them around their old stomping grounds while they argued about what happened where. We often found ourselves on the trail of the moonshiners. They left a network of trails and camps that ran from the tidewater dock at the town of Dungeness far into the mountains packing grain, sugar and yeast to supply the many thirsty mines, logging camps, fishing lodges, hunting camps, bawdy houses and homesteads that used to populate this last frontier.

In 1897 much of the Moonshiner's home range was declared a National Monument to protect the elk. This brought law to the Olympic Peninsula. 1920 brought Prohibition which as Will Rogers said, was "better than no liquor at all." There were conflicts. "Dodger Bender" manned the fire lookout on the mountain that now bears his name. The story goes that Dodger discovered a still and got knifed and killed by a moonshiner.

The rich farmlands of the Dungeness provided the grain that when combined with pure Olympic mountain spring water could supply an expanding market that the summer maneuvers of U.S. Navy's Pacific in the Port Angeles harbor represented. That was until 1933 when the do-gooders ended Prohibition and killed the moonshiners market. In 1938 the National Park took over, putting the last nail in the moonshiner's coffin. Today there's nothing much left of the moonshiners but a bunch of overgrown trails. The remains of a pioneer still are not much to look at. Just a collection of rusty metal barrel hoops sticking out of the forest floor. Other times you might see an old ten-gallon milk can. These were "borrowed" from dairy farms in the lowlands. Milk cans could serve a double purpose. With tight fitting metal lids, milk cans were the original bear and mouse proof container for packing supplies in and you could rig them to packing liquids out. It's an odd feeling to find dairy cans in the bottom of a timbered canyon where they tell a story few people know.

What my old friends didn't know about the Dungeness country wasn't worth knowing. Harry and Boone were the last of the mountain men, self-described reprobates and moonshine connoisseurs. They had hunted, fished, trapped, logged and guided this country for decades before I was born. They were living historic monuments. My job was to remember everything Harry and Boone said before they died. I had to remember, I didn't have a tape recorder. I couldn't write it down. Writing is impossible while you're bouncing down a steep logging road that you're not sure you can make it back up and your guides are arguing over which way to turn and carrying on a running battle over the names of every creek, hollow and knob along the way.

Geographic place names are a record of the past. Graveyard Spit was named after a massacre. Whiskey Flats was named after the town's leading industry. Wildcat Creek was named after one of Boone's old girlfriends. That's what Harry said anyway.

The day Harry's had his heart attack I was driving up a ridge where the big bucks moved in to feed on the mushrooms sprouted in the fall rains. Harry had his Long Tom, a single shot twelve-gauge shotgun that fed his family. Boone had a rifle that looked like a piece of lever-action scrap metal. He claimed to have got two elk with it. He said they were big five-point bulls, one at the head of Lost River and the other was up the Lillian River. These are remote tributaries of the upper Elwha, now deep within Olympic National Park. Boone and his father hunted and guided up there before there was a Park. They built the first trails and cabins now long destroyed. Boone offered to draw me a map of his old hunting country in his own style, with the letters backwards so I would have to look at it in a mirror to read it. I thought a map like that would be worth a fortune just for all the antique whiskey bottles you'd find around where the cabins stood but Boone died before he drew that map.

Now it looked like Harry was going to quit my research project. He still wanted to go fishing. It was February. The Dungeness was loaded with steelhead. I drove Harry up the river instead of to a hospital. I felt like an accomplice to fishing assisted suicide.

No fishing trip with Harry was really just a fishing trip. He was on a treasure hunt. That's why he brought the metal detector along. Harry found all kinds metal tools and stove parts buried under the sod of long abandoned homesteads. This was not an accepted method of surveying archaeological remains but I was in a hurry. Many of these homesteads were soon to be obliterated by real estate developments and a logging industry that had no appreciation for cultural resources. Harry was my guide to this lost world, a walking, talking treasure map with a metal detector.

Harry was convinced that treasure was buried on the Olympic Peninsula. In 1579 Francis Drake sailed past here in his ship, The Golden Hind after looting the Spanish of treasure they had looted from the Incas. It is generally accepted that Drake buried 17 tons of treasure somewhere to lighten the ship before crossing the Pacific Ocean in his circumnavigation of the globe. Harry thought he knew where the treasure was buried. I told Harry I would do the digging. All he had to do was say where. Following his directions, we found the probable location of the treasure, in an Indian graveyard. That made sense. Drake was a pirate. They often buried treasure with the dead who were left to guard it. That stopped the treasure hunt. We looked for another.

The Olympic Mountains contain very little gold. The gold that has been found here was thought to be brought by the continental ice sheet and deposited when the glaciers melted. A Frenchman allegedly found one of these placer deposits. He must have wandered into Dungeness or Blyn once too often with a bag of gold dust. Legend has it someone may have followed him back to the mine or maybe just found the mine by accident. The Frenchman was alarmed and disappeared. There was a large explosion. The entrance to the mine was obliterated. The Frenchman was never seen again. Harry thought he knew the location of the mine but if he was having another stroke and he probably wouldn't be doing much hiking in the rough country upriver. I was hoping he'd spill the beans before he kicked the bucket. Maybe he could have shown me the trail to the mine while we were fishing.

We made it to the river. It was still raining. Harry sat down on a log and rigged up his fishing gear. He talked about his faith which I thought was odd because we hadn't talked about God much. Harry said he didn't go to church in town. His church was the river, the woods and in the mountains. That was okay by me but what about the gold mine? I was just about to ask when Harry saw a fish roll. Harry tottered to the water's edge. Obviously, the stroke, the smokehouse and Lena's bath would have to wait. I walked upstream and turned back to watch Harry catch his last steelhead. The next day Harry had a stroke and we never fished again. One by one my old friends died and the Dungeness History Project was concluded.

31

THE WOODEN BOAT FESTIVAL.

It's time once again for the annual Port Townsend Wooden Boat Festival. I think it's about time Port Townsend had something to celebrate. The place had fallen on hard times since shortly after it was built. Port Townsend was once the official port of entry for all vessels entering Puget Sound. Then Port Townsend lost the customs house to Port Angeles. She still dreamed of becoming the terminus for a transcontinental railroad. The fact that Port Townsend was on the edge of the mountainous Olympic Peninsula, surrounded on three sides by treacherous bodies of water did nothing to dampen the spirit of her pioneer railroad boosters. It was common knowledge that all you needed was a little hard work and a lot of risk capital to lure the railroads to town. Port Townsend did not become the transcontinental terminus. The town had a hard time recovering. Betty MacDonald described Port Townsend in her 1945 epic, "The Egg and I" as "A barren old maid of a place, aged and weathered by all the prevailing winds and shunned by prosperity ... a dreary thing of empty buildings, pocked by falling bricks and tenanted only by rats and the winds." Betty was a heck of a writer but she never would have made it in real estate sales.

Lately Port Townsend has emerged as a wooden boat building center with a school and support industries. Building a boat may well be the highest and best use for a piece of wood. The Port Townsend Wooden Boat festival is keeping this tradition alive. There are few things I enjoy more than gazing at the graceful lines of a wooden boat. Once upon a time, to prove my love of wooden boats, I actually built one myself. This is not something I would recommend to anyone.

Building a wooden boat is no more complicated than say, rebuilding the engine in your automobile except for one small detail. If you forget to tighten a nut here or a bolt there and your engine blows up, you can just pretend you ran out of gas and walk home. If you build a wooden boat and it sinks, say at a crowded public boat ramp on a Saturday morning where everyone is waiting for you to salvage the wreck so they can launch, it can be very embarrassing even if you do survive. Building a wooden boat calls for an exceptional level of woodworking skills that require years of experience to master. In addition, there are a lot of special tools, fittings and wooden boat building tricks that can make the job a whole lot easier. The first things you'll need to build a wooden boat are a lot of those little metal pointy things with the flat top on one end. That's what holds your wooden boat together. Next, you'll need a chunk of metal mounted on a wood handle to bash the pointy metal things into the wood. It helps if your metal basher has a claw thing on it in case you pound stuff in the wrong place and have to rip it all out again. It happens.

It is at this point that a bit of caution is advised in the building of your wooden boat. To pound the pointy metal things into the wood, you must grasp them between your thumb and forefinger and hit them with the metal basher. It is at this crucial moment that you will miss and bash your thumb. When building a wooden boat its safety first. You'll want a deluxe first aid kit handy with plenty of field dressings and pain medications on hand. You may have to cut the wood while building a wooden boat. How you do that is your own business. I prefer a saw with a pull cord. Holding a piece of wood in one hand while cutting it with a chainsaw is a forgotten art that few wooden boat builders have mastered. Remember accuracy counts more than speed. Sometimes it's a good idea to measure the wood before you cut it. I recommend using one of those fancy thin, metal things with the little marks and numbers all over it. I sometimes wish I had one.

Next, you'll want to pay close attention to what you build your wooden boat out of. While building my wooden boat, I uncovered a dirty little secret about the wood boat building industry.

Do you know what wood boats are made of? They're made of wood and not just any wood either, nothing but the finest Alaskan yellow cedar and old growth Douglas fir. Using wood to build my wood boat was a lot of extra trouble but it was all worthwhile until the day I launched Gertie. She was named after the Press Expedition party barge that sank in the Elwha River during the hard winter of 1889. It's always a bad idea to name your wooden boat after another wooden boat that sank. I know that now. A hundred years later, the curse of the Gertie returned when my proud craft was bashed by the rocks of the upper Dungeness River, where she sank to her final resting place. Someday I'll build another wooden boat. I have to rebuild my engine first.

32

DEER SEASON - THIS COUNTRY SURE HAS GROWN UP.

Every year on the opening day of deer season I miss my old friend Clyde. We used to hunt together. For some people hunting is a sport but for us it was a way to get meat or go without. Clyde liked to drive logging roads and I liked to ride along. He was the best deer hunter I knew. Clyde always said something I did not understand when I was younger,

"This country sure has grown up." He was referring to the trees that grew back in the country after it was logged. Clyde had been a witness. His story reads like a history of the Olympic Peninsula. Born in in a logging camp at the Twin Rivers in the 1920's, Clyde was just in time for the Great Depression where his family survived by growing, shooting, catching, harvesting and preserving their own food. Nothing was wasted. Coming of age during the Depression, Clyde was just in time for World War Two where he joined the Coast Guard. While scraping paint on the boat he was sailing into the battle of the Aleutians, the Skipper told Clyde to take it easy or he'd poke a hole in the old rust-bucket. After the Aleutians Clyde went south for the invasion of the Philippines. After the war Clyde came home and commercial fished, logged and built logging bridges all over the Peninsula. He was of what we call, "The Greatest Generation." He gave us a lifetime of historical perspectives like when he showed up at a logging show in the early 80's where we were busy untangling a mass of wire rope with a sledgehammer and a metal wedge.

"This looks like the last Depression." Clyde chuckled. One day he showed us how to blast logs apart for easier yarding. In what I regard as the single bravest act I ever saw in the woods, he beat a hollow iron wedge full of gunpowder into a log and lit the fuse. Then he just stood there while I hid behind a root wad. After several dud fuses the gunpowder wedge went off blowing the log into kindling sticks.

Once while we were deer hunting we came upon a logging show with the tower set up right in the middle of the road. I suggested we turn around and get out of there but Clyde had no use for back seat drivers. In what I consider the second bravest act I ever saw in the woods, Clyde walked up to the yarder and asked the crew to move it so we could get by. The loggers said no. Clyde got mad explaining how the yarder was on tracks. They could have just slacked off on the tail hold a couple of feet and we'd still be hunting.

Then his eyes went bad, his heart went gunnysack and the injuries from work caught up to him. It was hard to get him out of the house. I remember Clyde's last hunt. He didn't even want to go hunting so I shot a deer for him and braced it up with a forked stick so it looked like it was bedded down. Then I went and called Clyde and told him the deer were really running. In fact, I could practically guarantee him a nice buck. He stalked into the meadow, saw the deer and chewed me out in words you cannot print in a newspaper. It's illegal to shoot another guy's deer. It was stupid. Clyde was scrupulously legal in all of his hunting, fishing clamming and crabbing. I had offended the pride and honor of my oldest, best hunting buddy but I thought it was the least I could do at the time. Thirty-five years later Clyde, the meadow, the roads we used to drive and the game we used to hunt are gone. This country has sure grown up.

33

HALLOWEEN – THE MILLION DOLLAR MULE.

I heard the rumble of the mule truck at midnight. That's when I remembered I should have gotten ready for the big packing job. I'd never ridden a mule before so when I was offered the chance of wrangling on a mule train I jumped at the chance. It sounded like a dream vacation come true. We were off on an October elk hunt to the Bitterroot Mountains, a range Captain Lewis of the Lewis and Clark Expedition called the "most terrible mountains I ever beheld." The Bitterroots were said to be inhabited by a tribe Lewis called "the broken mocerssons." They lived in caves, stole horses and ate them raw. I thought they might have a casino by now.

"It's good elk country, but there's lots of grizzly bears," the mule skinner said. Given the choice between a mule and a grizzly I'm not sure which animal I fear most. Either one of them will kill you but the mule will let you pet them first. None of that mattered when we pulled into the trail head after an all-night drive. We let the mules out of the stock trailer. The smell was terrific. I thought we should take the mules to a carwash but before I could collect my wits or locate the restroom facilities I was handed the end of a rope that was tied to the most terrifying creature I ever saw in the woods.

"Here's your mule," the mule skinner said. "Be careful. He's been to Mule College. He's worth $5,000." That hurt. Not only was the mule better educated than I was, he was worth more. He was a long-legged, razor-backed, brindle-coated mule that must have stood more than six feet high at the top of his shoulder. His head was even higher than that. I tried to remember everything I knew about mules. You are supposed to show the mule who is boss. I started feeding the mule marshmallows. After the bag was gone we started in on a box of donuts. So far, the mule ride was going well but I still had to get on him. We ran out of donuts. The mule started to fidget. The rest of the mules where headed up the trail. I jumped for the saddle and made it half way up the mule when he took off down the trail to catch up with his friends. We skidded to a stop against the rump of another mule that had stopped in the middle of the trail to survey the first obstacle. It was a swinging bridge suspended with cables over a river. Once the lead animal started across the bridge the rest of the mules followed. The bridge started bouncing. It was like riding a mule on a trampoline. The six of us, three mules, a horse and two riders made it across the bridge and started switch-backing up the ridge on a steep and narrow trail. I wondered what would happen if we met another pack string but we never did.

There were a lot of downed trees that had fallen across the trail. Someone had cut them out of the way but when a pack on one of the mules snagged the end of a cut wind fall, it slid across the trail like a runaway telephone pole narrowly missing me and my mule. We went over the side of the mountain together to dodge the log. I thought this would be a good time to get off but before I could bail, the mule bounced back on the trail. Right then I figured the mule was worth ten thousand dollars. One end of the runaway log still blocked the trail. I thought it was just a good thing I'd brought an axe along. I got off the mule and set to work chopping the log. My mule was not about to wait for me to chop the log with the rest of his friends disappearing up the trail. He jumped over me and the log and took off up the trail at a gallop. I ran to catch up. It's a bad mistake to run with an axe or be in a hurry around mules. I came around a sharp bend in the trail and startled the mules all over again. They might have trampled my friend if he hadn't stopped them with a sheer force of will. Once everyone calmed down I climbed back on the monster's back. I thought we could just relax and go for a ride, but I still had a lot to learn about mules. Riding at the rear of the string I had little or no idea what was happening ahead. Once we stopped at a narrow part of the trail above a cliff where I could not see the bottom. The mule in front of me was said to have a lot of personality, which means the same with mules as it does with people. He was a real pain. The mule craned its neck and turned to look me in the eye then kicked my mule square in the chest, again and again. My mule just stood there and took it. By then I figured the mule was worth a million dollars. That was the finest riding animal I had ever been on. He had a long stride and a smooth gait. If there was a log across the trail he couldn't just step over he would jump it. Still, no mule is perfect. The pack string stopped in the trail and wouldn't budge. All ears pointed to the same brushy hillside. After a while the brushy hillside moved. It wasn't a hillside at all but a pair of moose that looked to be the size of a mountain. The mules were terrified. They took off at a gallop and did not slow down until they bogged down in a patch of muskeg. By the time we pulled the mules out of the swamp they were really ready for the car wash. It was getting dark. We found a nice patch of grass by a creek and made camp. That's when I found this mule's weak point. He did not like to be tied up. He spent the night snorting and digging a hole to China with his front hooves which made for very little sleep that night.

At daylight, a low moaning sound came from the woods. It was the mating call of the bull moose. He must have fallen in love with the mules who were not interested. I tried to calm my mule down with candy bars and espresso. After a while the moose went away. The mules calmed down and went to sleep. After all, they had been up all night. I figured if I kept them awake during the day, they might try sleeping at night. I hobbled the mule and turned him loose to feed. That was a mistake. The mule had no trouble galloping away, not bothered in the least by the hobbles. The great elk hunt had just become the great mule hunt. I took off down the valley, cursing and tracking the mule until the tracks ran out in the thick timber. After a while I came to a meadow. There was a small tent city on the edge of the timber. It was an outfitter's camp. I could only imagine how glad they would be to see some tourists horn in on his hunting country. Being lost was no excuse. We had violated the law of those hills by unknowingly camping too close to another outfit. Then my mule got loose and I didn't even have a lead rope to fetch him back with. I felt like a total greenhorn but then again, I was.

Just then I spotted my mule. He was a nosing a stack of feed sacks. I saw someone walk out of the woods about a hundred yards away. He was a strange looking guy who looked like an old- time mountain man, dressed in fringed buckskin with a big floppy hat with feathers in it. He walked up behind the mule with a rope.

"This ought to be good," I thought. I waited for the rodeo but the mule never even looked sideways. He followed the old guy over to the hitching post, got tied up and for once did not throw a fit about it. I walked over to the mule. He looked bored. I wanted to thank the old guy and ask him how he tied up the mule without an argument but he had disappeared. I lead the mule back to camp. We saddled up and spent the day riding on elk trails through the Bitterroots. It was one of the most breathtaking experiences I have ever had but we did not see a single elk. That evening I rode by the outfitter's camp to return the lead rope. There were horses in the corral and smoke coming from the stove in the cook tent. Someone was at home. He came out of the tent wearing a pistol. I explained how my mule got away and the old guy caught him with the lead rope and I was bringing it back.

"What old guy?" the outfitter asked. "There's nobody here but me. The wranglers, the cook and all my guides just up and quit. They claim the place is haunted. Nobody will spend the night here."

"Who cares if it's haunted," I said trying to look on the bright side. "There aren't any elk here."

"Don't you think I know that? And I've got six elk hunters showing up tomorrow. I don't know what I'm going to do," he said, nervously tugging at a bottle in his vest. I felt sorry for the guy and guilty for cramping his outfit. I offered to blow an elk call every once in a while. Maybe his clients would think there were elk in the valley.

"Would you?" the outfitter gushed. "I'd make it worth your while."

"I don't want to get shot," I said with emphasis.

"Don't worry," the outfitter said. "My hunters never hit anything they shoot at."

Reassured, I rode away thinking I'd gotten off easy. The next morning, we took down our camp at daylight, loaded the mules and left the haunted valley.

34

HALLOWEEN – THE TELL-TALE TAIL – WITH APOLOGIES TO EDGAR ALLAN POE.

Fog season is my favorite time of year. Whether it is an effect of global warming or a shift in ocean currents, the fog has been especially thick this year. For fog worshippers, this is the perfect opportunity for a fog-drenched vacation to a hidden land of shadows. Finding your own personal fog bank should not be a problem. Unlike a sunny vacation where crowds can be a hassle you can get lost in the fog. Other fog fans will not intrude on your solitude. You won't be able to see them. In really big fog events you won't be able to see the hand in front of your face. The health benefits of fog are only just now being discovered while exposure to the sun can cause dangerous skin burns. No one has ever gotten a fog burn. After a long hot summer of boring blue sky, we look forward to fog for a soothing protection from the sun's harmful rays.

I like fishing in the fog. It delays the twilight of dawn so the daylight bite can last all day long. One morning the fog was so thick you could cut it with a chainsaw. We launched in the river in the dark and floated into the vapors. The water and sky merged into one gray color. The sounds of the river were muffled and bent. The fog had sharpened my senses, not destroyed, nor dulled them. My hearing was acute. I heard all things on the river. Does that make me crazy? I think not. Observe how calmly I can tell this story. There were geese calling from somewhere downstream. There was the whistle of an elk and the roar of white water below. The river dropped over some big rocks in the foggy rapids that made it look like we were falling off the edge of the Earth. We may have been; nothing looked familiar.

The fog was so thick even the fish ducks were confused. They flew past our heads just swerving to miss us. Mergansers are a bird about the size of a football that can fly more than 40 miles an hour. To have a flock of these saw-billed missiles headed straight for your head so close you can feel the air from their wings is one of the most terrifying bird watching experiences you can have. Then a new anxiety seized me. I became aware of a large creature wading in the river below us. It walked on two legs. You could tell it was heavy by the way it clattered the rocks on the bottom of the river with its feet. The splashing stopped. Then came a shuffling sound accompanied by some rude grunting noises. It was coming closer. I anchored up and kept quite still. I lowered a herring in the water.

In almost no time we hooked a great fish. Whatever sort of monster was headed our way would have to wait. There in the murk of fog and twilight the great fish was brought aboard. Just my luck: It was a Dolly Varden, or bull trout. Nobody can tell the difference. Despite the fact that on any given day it might be the most prolific fish in the river, this member of the char family was declared an endangered species by the corrupt bureaucracies that mismanage our fisheries. The Dolly Varden or bull trout or whatever you choose to call it is a scavenger that feeds upon the young and spawn of salmon. Protecting the bull trout makes about as much sense as raising raccoons in your chicken house. Despite this, the Dolly Varden/bull trout is an MVP in one of the greatest horrors ever perpetrated on the American taxpayer: the extinction for profit industry. This is a collection of incompetent pencil-pushing functionaries whose every corrupt edict makes the fish more endangered. The more endangered the fish become, the more money is spent on them. It is a beautiful system, unless you fish.

Just catching a Dolly Varden/bull trout makes me so darned mad it makes me crazy. At what point has an endangered species, which was never actually a real species or endangered, considered to be recovered? If you catch 20 bull trout a day on a river, wouldn't that mean it is no longer endangered? I guess not. You cannot even lift a bull trout out of the water. That is insane! I am not insane I tell you! The fishing laws are insane! They make people crazy! Just reading the fishing laws is enough to give you Tourette syndrome. Have I not told you that what is often mistaken for madness is nothing more than an acute fishing problem?

I netted the bull trout and lifted it into the boat committing the perfect crime. I didn't want to eat it. I didn't want the fish for a trophy. No, maybe I went insane for a moment when the eye of the fish met mine. It was like looking into the eye of a vulture. I made up my mind to take the life of the fish and rid myself of the eye forever.

My psychologist said that clubbing fish was a transference issue so I punched him. I knew the fish well. I pitied the fish though. I knew it had been laying in that fishing hole all along just waiting to steal my bait. His fears had been ever growing since I dropped my anchor and lowered the gear. Then I raised my fish club and smacked the bull trout in the head. The tail of the fish slapped the deck one time and then another and then stopped altogether. Yes, he was stone, stone dead. I worked hastily and in silence, cutting off the head, removing the viscera and quickly depositing the body in my tackle box. When I had made an end to these labors, I heard a voice cry out, "Who's there?"

There came a figure out of the fog who introduced himself with perfect suavity. He was a fish cop. I smiled, for what had I to fear? I bade him welcome and invited him to search my humble craft. The officer was satisfied. My manner convinced him of my innocence. I talked more fluently but then heard something that made me pale and weak. He sat. We chatted. My head ached. What you mistake for madness is but an acuteness of my hearing. I was sure I could hear a low, quick sound such as a metronome might make when smeared with axle grease. It was the slapping of the tail of the bull trout from deep inside the tackle box coffin.

I gasped for breath. I became pale. I raved, I swore but the noise gained definitiveness. If the fish cop heard the noise, he must have ignored it. Then this hellish tattoo increased quicker and louder until I thought my head must burst! The fish cop knew, suspected and made a mockery of my horror until I could no longer bear the agony. I reached for my tackle box and shrieked, "Here y'are fish cop! I admit the deed! Here, here open my tackle box! It is the beating of the tell-tale tail!"

35

HALLOWEEN – BIGFOOT BEGONE

The Olympic Peninsula is one of the most popular locations in the nation to see a Sasquatch. This large, hairy, two-legged ape-like creature has haunted this land since the beginning. Every tribe on the Olympic Peninsula has its own story that describes the creature as everything from a Grendel-like cannibal ogre to a wise and gifted healer, depending on who you talk to. Founded in 1995, the Bigfoot Research Organization is a group of dedicated researchers, scientists, journalists and specialists from diverse backgrounds dedicated to studying this species in the field and the laboratory in an effort to derive conclusive evidence of the creature's existence through research and education in a way that does not harm the creature.

The BFRO records indicate that Washington State leads the country with 573 Sasquatch sightings. 79 of them were on the Olympic Peninsula! This relatively high population of Sasquatch has made the Peninsula a hotbed of Bigfoot research. Legions of dedicated researchers, investigators, biologists and trackers have committed themselves to documenting the existence of the Sasquatch in a non-invasive manner with respect and sensitivity through science and education without harming the creature in any way. Their goal is to obtain as much information and empirical evidence as possible through a comprehensive habitat study and DNA analysis with hopes of being prepared when and if species verification comes to fruition. Some dedicated researchers have placed game cameras in remote areas in hopes of photo-documenting this amazing creature without harming them in any way. The good news is that after all these years of dedicated research by these dedicated researchers, not one of these amazing creatures has been harmed in any way. In addition, the game cameras have recorded many picturesque shots of bear, elk, deer and mountain goats enjoying their native environment.

Fortunately, today's enlightened Bigfoot researchers have avoided the destructive process of discovery that would undoubtedly lead to the demise of this missing link with our past. Many creatures, from the 100-pound salmon to the Forks logger, have become extinct or endangered after they were discovered. Today's Sasquatch seekers have come to realize, through the DNA analysis of Sasquatch hair, droppings and nail clippings that what they used to call "the creature", the "monster" and "the missing link," is in fact human. They are large hairy humans but can't we celebrate diversity and accept others whose physical appearance may be different than our own? You would never think of calling a logger a "brush ape," to their face anyway so why is it okay to call the Sasquatch People "swamp monsters?" This startling new DNA evidence proves what the Native Americans have said all along. The Sasquatch are people. Still, Bigfoot Hunters want to prove the existence of the Sasquatch People so they can be protected but given our record of protecting other indigenous people, I'd head for the hills before I got discovered if I was a Sasquatch.

Now that they're considered human, the Sasquatch People have an opportunity to contribute to the fabric of our nation's economy. It's only fair now that the Sasquatch People have been accepted as human by the Sasquatch Researchers, the Sasquatch People should be able to purchase the same permits we all must have to be on public land. For example, if a family of four Sasquatch People wanted to go camping in Olympic National Park they would need either an annual or weekly pass in addition to back country use permits. The Sasquatch People would need to be aware of the Backcountry Reservation system and rent or purchase a bear proof canister where required by law. The budget minded Sasquatch People might try to go camping on State Land to beat the system but that would require a Discover Pass.

The important research of various Sasquatch researchers has also documented the Sasquatch People engaged in hunting deer, fishing and digging clams. Now that they have been proven to be human, the Sasquatch People should be required to acquire the same hunting, fishing, seaweed and shellfish licenses that allow the rest of us the privilege to harvest these resources. In addition, all Sasquatch People should obey our fish and game laws which means no more snacking on our iconic Olympic Marmots. With all of the licenses, permits and fees that are required to be human, the Sasquatch People would be advised to keep from being discovered as long as humanly possible. Which begs the question. How can you protect yourself from something that is not known to exist?

Almost every year someone disappears in the vast wilderness of the Olympic Peninsula without a trace. When all other missing person explanations fail the Sasquatch are inevitably blamed which is blatantly unfair but you never know. The main goal of the Sasquatch hunter should be to avoid becoming Sasquatch bait. Many of the so-called Sasquatch hunters are just asking for trouble by carrying firearms in case of Sasquatch attack. Shooting a critter as big and mean as a grizzly could make them mad if they found out about it. Then it's like they said on the frontier: Save the last bullet for yourself. Bear repellant runs the grizzly off without harm to the bear or human. Sasquatch repellant works on the same proven principle and besides, shooting the Sasquatch could jeopardize future opportunities for observation and social interaction with the creature. More successful primate researchers have employed an alternative methodology.

The famed archaeologist Louis Leakey thought he could gain insights into the origins of human behavior by studying the great apes with a team of attractive alpha females that became known as "Leakey's Angels." Jane Goodall studied chimpanzees. Diane Fossey studied mountain gorillas. Birute Galdikas studied orangutans. Leakey said women made better primate researchers because males are seen as domineering power-mongers while females were perceived to be the less threatening peacemakers in ape societies. "Leakey's Angels" never packed guns or collected a specimen of the great apes. They spent years gaining the creatures trust by sitting still and mingling among the apes with submissive body language. Eye contact is seen as aggressive behavior in primates. Conversely the average Sasquatch hunter's tool kit includes binoculars, cameras and heat-sensor things that are off-putting to sensitive wilderness creatures, myself included. As for carrying firearms, even a grouse can tell if a man is carrying a gun. To study any animal closely you must gain its trust. Unfortunately, gaining the trust of a Sasquatch could prove fatal for the Sasquatch researcher. That's where an effective Sasquatch repellant could come in handy.

As a fishing guide, I was getting fed up with my clients being frightened by these terrifying creatures. Rowing a drift boat down our rainforest rivers fishing for salmon and steelhead is tough enough. Try floating down the river in the pre-dawn darkness with trees and rocks falling around and a loud screaming coming out of the woods. Typically, the clients start babbling:

"There's something out there!" That's when I try to reassure them that the Sasquatch couldn't possibly exist. Because if people only knew how many Sasquatch were actually on the Olympic Peninsula they would not come here for a vacation and I would be out of business. That's why I invented Bigfoot Begone™, a hypoallergenic, carbon-neutral, gluten-free Sasquatch repellant. Why gamble on the safety of your family and loved ones when for the price of a box of buckshot you can treat an area the size of a football field with Bigfoot Begone, a guide-tested, mom-approved method of removing these dangerous pests.

Bigfoot Begone might cost a little more than your drug store Sasquatch repellants, but what is the price of a good night's sleep? Can you put a price on the safety and security of your family and loved ones on your next outdoor adventure? But wait there's more! Bigfoot Begone is now available in a handy aerosol spray that is guaranteed to not harm the ozone layer. In fact, we're so sure Bigfoot Begone will work that if you think you see a Sasquatch while using this product simply return the unused portion and we'll cheerfully refund your money. Bigfoot Begone eliminates the need to save the last bullet for yourself. Get some Bigfoot Begone today.

36

OPENING DAY OF ELK SEASON
– THE GRANDMA PIE.

Of the many things that I love about elk hunting, it's the nightly buffet at the elk hunting camp that I enjoy most. By elk hunting I don't mean driving around in the suburbs hunting someone's pet elk. No, I do my elk hunting out in the rainforest, where the elk are as wild as the country. It can rain several inches every day. Throw in some wind, hail and lightning, and your camping trip becomes a survival mission. After the first day in elk camp you don't care what you eat. Whether it's a chili dog rolled in gravel, bear knuckle stew or a burnt on the outside-raw-on-the-inside hamburger between two pieces of moldy bread, fine dining in the elk camp can be an interesting experience.

Once we had to fire an elk camp cook for adding the wrong wild mushrooms to the chili and testing the punch to the point where dinnertime found our chef laying by the fire in a light rainforest sprinkle. When one side of the cook started steaming from the heat of the fire we rolled him over to dry the other side. That's what I enjoy most about elk hunting. It's the comradery and of course Grandma's apple pie. Grandma had given me a pie to take out to the elk camp. It had something to do with one of the hunters fixing her car. It was sort of a payback, with interest really. The value of a Grandma pie in a wilderness full of elk camps would soar beyond belief, especially if you had some vanilla ice cream to go with it. Not that I would ever sell a Grandma pie. It was beyond price. That's why it was too bad the muzzle of my rifle accidentally punched a hole in the top crust of the pie while it was sitting on the seat of my truck. Imagine dropping a broken bottle through the smile of the Mona Lisa. That's how I felt after blemishing the Grandma pie.

There was only one thing to do, I mean two. I had to clean the pie out of my rifle before opening morning, but I had to take care of the pie first. I cut a wedge of pie from around the imprint of the rifle barrel. It was a little slice of heaven. I made a real mess of cutting that first wedge. It was crooked so I cut another one trying to do a proper job of it. After all, Grandma's pies don't grow on trees. Then it was lunch time and how could I not have a piece of pie for lunch? Later I noticed the pie was still out of alignment. It just looked all wrong so I made a perfect cut straight across the pan. Half the pie was gone.

Then I imagined the abuse I'd take back at the elk camp for eating half a pie by myself, especially from the poor sucker who had worked on Grandma's car. There was nothing left to do but eat the rest of the pie. When it was gone, I decided to bake another pie in Grandma's now empty pie pan just to make up for eating the whole thing by myself. I soaked some dried apples in beer and put the mixture between two tortillas, baked the mess and announced the pie was ready. Everyone seemed to like it. There were no complaints, but then it was an elk camp where pie is pie, and no matter how you slice it, it's better than no pie at all.

37

ELECTION DAY.

"The whole country is going to hell in a bucket and now we've just elected that idiot for president!" my fancy friend shrieked the day after Election Day.

"Which idiot is that?" I asked, pretending to care. There's nothing like talking politics to ruin a perfectly good fall day floating down a river catching salmon. When you're hooked up to a big king salmon you don't care who the president is but once the fishing gets slow people get bored and start bad-mouthing the president no matter who it is.

America is a nation of law. I don't make the rules but I try to follow them. Similarly, there are rules at the fish camp that allow a free discourse of opposing ideas about the cuisine, the weather and the estimated weight of a fish while preserving a civilized decorum of relaxation and good taste. I like to celebrate diversity as much as the next guy. Heck, we have even let a fly fisherman into the fish camp in the name of burying the hatchet on the row vs. wade controversy. Fly fishermen wade the river. I row a boat down the river. Can't we all get along? The first rule in any fish camp is: no arguments before breakfast. Chances are if you wait until after breakfast you'll forget what you were arguing about. Rule number two: No bear meat in the chili contest. That should be self-explanatory.

The final and possibly most important rule at the fish camp is: no politics. Start talking politics in the fish camp and you are gone. Politics has always been a nasty business. Aristophanes said it best when he summed up what constitutes a popular politician: "a horrible voice, bad breeding and a vulgar manner." Since then the abuse of politicians has become the great American pastime where we conveniently forget we voted these people into office in the first place and keep them there until they are rich and old. You think we bad-mouth politicians now but it's nothing compared to the good old days. George Washington was the father of our country. President Washington's terms in office were not a honeymoon in Camelot. President Washington had an enemies list as long as your arm.

Fortunately, these events occurred in a period of our history when journalists had a command of the English language. James Thomson Callender, a reporter for The Richmond Recorder fled his native Scotland in 1793 to avoid sedition charges based on his writing and settled in the newly formed United States. Callender called President Washington "the grand lama of the federal adoration, the immaculate divinity of Mount Vernon." Callender described our second president, John Adams, as a "hideous hermaphroditical character, which has neither the force nor firmness of a man, nor the gentleness and sensibility of a woman." Callender accused Adams of wanting to crown himself king. Adams responded by charging Callender with sedition. Callender was fined $200 and jailed for nine months until the last day of Adams' administration, when the Sedition Act expired and Thomas Jefferson took over and set him free. In return, Callender wrote: "it would have been best to have Jefferson "beheaded five minutes before his inaugural address."

Callender reported in a series of articles that Jefferson fathered children by his slave Sally Hennings. While historians traditionally refuted the charge, DNA analysis and historical evidence concluded that Callender's accusations were indeed true, about two hundred years later. Destitute and drunk, Callender was found drowned in three feet of water in the James River in Virginia after apparently falling in, proving that even in the best of times journalism can be a risky business.

Not much has changed since the time of our founding fathers. We are still using in the Electoral College, a system designed for isolated, semi-literate white male farmers living on the far-flung reaches of the frontier. At the end of the day I think we can all be proud that the voters that bothered to vote elected the best politicians money can buy. I say if it ain't fixed don't break it.

38

VETERANS FISHING DAY.

I never set out to be a fishing guide. When I was a kid I wanted to be the president of the United States of America. What kid wouldn't want to be president? This is a country where you can do whatever it is you want and anything can happen. It might have happened to me except for one thing, the fourth grade. That's when they started with the new math. They said pie are square and that's not right. Berry cobblers and rhubarb crisp are square. Pies are round. The government probably keeps this information secret for a reason but long story short, I did not become president. I am a fishing guide.

When I first applied to fishing guide school I knew it would be a rough road where only the tough survived. I had no obvious tattoos or piercings. There were no warrants out for my arrest. I was not currently enrolled in a court-ordered substance abuse or anger management program. No restraining orders had been issued against me. I was polite, reasonable and efficient. I didn't drink, chew, spit, smoke, cuss, or lie. I didn't tell dirty jokes or play practical jokes. They let me have a fishing guide license anyway. My motto was, fake it till you make it. I faked getting bites just to make people think they had a fish on. I faked being a relationship and career counselor which was tough for an unemployed hermit. After a while I lacked the emotional commitment to fake it. I was going to quit fishing altogether but people kept calling me. Like Bob Gooding of Olympic Sporting Goods in Forks. Bob is the official Forks fishing guru and life coach with a heart as big as Forks and Forks is a big-hearted town. Bob wanted me to take some veterans fishing. All the really good fishing guides must have been busy. I didn't care. Taking veterans fishing is the best thing I do. I used to take World War II veterans fishing. They were the greatest generation that beat the Axis Powers. Then I fished the Korean War veterans who were surrounded and said that was okay, they could attack in any direction. I fished the Vietnam veterans who served their country with distinction and were often disrespected when they came home.

These days I fish veterans who've survived years of war in a searing sandbox of horror. It is an honor to catch fish for people who have sacrificed so much for our country. That morning I showed up for the heart-stopper breakfast in Forks, where from previous experience I knew it's best to glom on to the smallest guys in the room. It's a case of the lighter the better when you're rowing folks down the river. Some of the beefcake fishermen weighed as much as my two guys put together who would not have weighed over 150 pounds apiece soaking wet in leaky boots. It was an observation that did not go unnoticed by my fellow professionals, whose uncharitable remarks only hinted at their regrets of not having thought of it first.

It was a recipe for mayhem. Take a dozen fishing guides. Put them in a small room. Add liquid and stir it up. Sensing we should rapidly deploy to get the first water, I showed the troops an important wilderness survival tip by stuffing my pockets with chunks of bacon wrapped up in a hotcake for an iron ration that could last many days if cured properly. We got a box lunch to go along with it with potato chips. I told the troops we could use the chips for fire starter once it started raining. To which they responded: "Rain?" They had no idea rain might be a very real possibility in the rainforest. I reassured the troops that it seldom rained here but in the unlikely event we should encounter a penetrating drizzle we had them covered with plenty of spare rain gear.

Somewhat reassured by the impossibility of rain, the troops revealed the true purpose of their mission. Their sergeant told them to catch a salmon or don't come back. The pressure was on. I explained how they should have been here 100 years ago if they wanted to catch a salmon. How all the salmon these days are threatened, endangered or just plain gone. It's all part of an insidious system of client hazing rituals that should have been banned by the Geneva Convention of Fishing years ago, where people are brainwashed to believe the fish are extinct so a guide looks like a genius if they catch one.

Once we were on the river another guide passed us with a vindictive flurry of unbelievably inappropriate comments which revealed a deep-seated inability to get over it. He pulled in front of us to a fishing hole just downstream that I had my eye on. I explained to the troops how we were being low-holed. This, after all I had done for the other guide, bailing him out of reform school and teaching him to write numbers so he could fill out his punch card. Then disaster struck. With a merry cry of "fish on!" a big salmon jumped in front of the other boat.

Now the low-holer was showboating by hooking a fish right as we passed by just for revenge. It was humiliating. I sure hope all the best guides aren't too busy for the next Veterans Day fishing trip. Our veterans deserve the best.

39

THE LAST DAY OF HUNTING SEASON – ROAD HUNTING WITH GRANNY.

And so another hunting season passes astern. I hope your season went better than mine. It was a washed-up shipwreck of failure and blame. Things started out okay. I read a lot of outdoor magazines on how to get ready for deer season. I watched a number of low-budget hunting videos that stressed the importance of set-up, execution and being on a private ranch where you can shoot baited deer like rats at the dump from the comfort of your heated blind. That sounded good to me but deer hunting on the Olympic Peninsula is seldom like that. I used to enjoy good deer hunting in the Olympic Mountains but that has been ruined. I blame the government. By failing to address global warming they have allowed the glaciers to melt. The decreasing weight of the glaciers has caused the Olympic Mountains to rise and become much steeper and higher lately. Hunting the lowlands is no picnic either. I had some equipment failures. I tried some of the new hunting clothes that trap human odors inside so they don't leak out and spook the deer. Combining an odor-trapping suit with a double helping of deer camp chili is a recipe for disaster.

The last day of deer season found me driving around looking like a pumpkin in an orange vest. That's how you can spot the real losers. Hunters are legally required to wear tacky orange accessories. It makes them easier for the game wardens to spot. Anyone still wearing hunter orange on the last day of the season is a dud as a hunter. It was okay. Hunting is all about family to me. On the last Sunday of deer season, I went and sprang Granny from the care center. I told the warden we were going to church. Granny didn't care where she was going as long as it was out on the road. She didn't seem to mind when I told her we were going to do a little road hunting through the suburbs of the Dungeness Valley on the way to church.

"I thought people went hunting in the woods," Granny said.

"Too many poachers in the woods," I said. Then I told her about the glaciers melting and how the woods were getting too steep to walk around in anymore, but Granny never cared much about science. Just then I spotted a trophy deer. It was a three point if you counted the nose and both ears, bedded down in someone's front yard in between a boat and an RV. I told Granny to go knock on their door and ask them if they could move their boat and RV so her "Sonny" could shoot the deer. I told her to tell them they were running low on fresh meat back at the home or something. Granny thought that was a bad idea, until I said we could go to the casino once I got my deer. What was I supposed to do? Ask for permission to hunt myself? Take a look at me. Now picture a cute little granny all dolled up in her Sunday-go-to-meeting best. Who is more likely to get permission to hunt? There's a hunting tip you won't get in any outdoor magazine. Unfortunately, there's a lot of anti-hunter attitude out there. I didn't get my deer. I took Granny to the casino anyway. She won enough money to buy me a steak.

ILLUSTRATIONS

1. The Trail to Marmot Country

2. Polly

3 Best Fishing Buddy.

4. Western Red Cedar

5. Skunk Cabbage

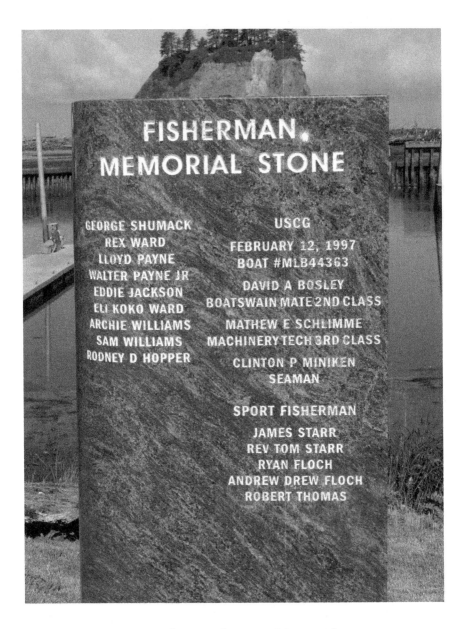

6. Quileute Fisherman Memorial

7. Fish Camp.

8. Deer Plotting Revenge.

9. Humes Ranch

10. Tree Falling Ahead

11. The Bull Trout

12. Thanksgiving.

13. Opening Day of Steelhead Season.

14. Hoh River Steelhead

15. Mom Could See the Need for Long Range Bombers.

40

THANKSGIVING.

Lately someone asked me how you can give thanks in hard times. Just think back to the first Thanksgiving. Do you think that was a pleasure cruise? More than a hundred pilgrims left England in September of 1620 on a scurvy voyage that was so rough the Mayflower nearly split in half. It took until November to sail the 3,000 miles across the Atlantic to the New World. By then the snow was falling. The pilgrims were so hungry they had to rob an Indian grave for food.

According to the pilgrims, they landed on Plymouth Rock seeking religious freedom. That meant among other things the right to read the Bible in English, hang witches and steal land from the Indians. Colonizing the New World was hard work that could give you quite an appetite. It turned out there was more to pioneering than just robbing graves and stealing land. You had to plant something. It had to grow. By the end of the first year the pilgrims were sick and starving. Half of them died in the first winter. The Indians had plenty of food. The Indians taught the pilgrims how to harvest maple syrup, plant corn and smoke meat. As a way of thanking the Indians, the pilgrims wiped them off the face of the earth. The American historian and wit Will Rogers once estimated it took one round of ammunition for every acre the Pilgrims settled. Rogers should know. He said, "My ancestors didn't come over on the Mayflower, they met the boat."

There was seldom a shortage of ammunition on the frontier.

After settling the eastern seaboard, the pilgrims headed west to make Thanksgiving a symbol of America that we celebrate to this day. It is the story of the American Manifest Destiny, the belief that God gave us this land.

The pilgrims knew what to do with it. They chopped down the forest and planted corn, cotton and tobacco amid the stumps until the soil wore out then loaded up and headed west looking for new land. The inexorable tide of westward expansion bluffed the English, French, Russians and Spanish from sea to shining sea giving us a much different country than the pilgrims could ever have dreamed of.

Thanksgiving is a good time to give thanks to the Indians. We should be glad they were nothing at all like the pilgrims. We should be thankful we are not pilgrims. That we live in a push-button era of automatic time-saving devices with no payments until next year.

Thanksgiving is a chance to get together with beloved dysfunctional family members and seasonally depressed friends to catch up on the latest news and gossip about anyone who doesn't happen to be around at the time. Thanksgiving means more to me than a mindless carnival of gluttony and excess where I load my plate higher and higher until I can't eat one more bite of chicken-fried fudge, passing out in front of the television with one eye propped open to watch as yet another ball game drags our system of higher education into the gutter. Thanksgiving is everything. The ability to appreciate the good and the bad, the things you have and the things you don't, that is Thanksgiving to me.

41

DECEMBER 1 – THE OPENING DAY OF STEELHEAD SEASON.

The end of salmon season was like the end of a lot of things: a sudden surprise that left me in shock. It was the day my universe came crashing down. It seems as only yesterday the maple trees were flowering and we were fishing the spring Chinook. Then as the days grew hotter, the summer Coho appeared. The rains of autumn brought the fall run of kings and silvers back up the rivers to spawn. We saw the leaves turn color and blow away leaving the trees like skeletons in the sky. We watched great flocks of migrating birds fly south but it all happened too fast. You lose track of time when you're fishing for salmon. It's a theory of relativity thing. A person can go to a job they hate and one shift will seem to last for three days. The same person can start salmon fishing at daylight then act confused when it seems to be getting dark.

"That's because the sun went down," I explain. Call it a coincidence or a guide's intuition but it gets mighty dark when that happens. It's all part of being a guide – to share the wisdom of years of experience on the river in a way that catches fish. Without the salmon, my life had no meaning. Each day became a long dreary exercise that stretched to a limitless bleak horizon with absolutely no possibility of catching a fish. That's when it hit me: The end of salmon season is the beginning of steelhead season! It just goes to show how fishing can be like life. About the time one boat sinks another one floats by to pick you up.

December first is the traditional opening day of winter steelhead season. If you don't know what a steelhead is you're probably better off not knowing. Steelhead are rainbow trout that are born in a river then migrate out to the ocean. Just like the salmon, the steelhead return to the rivers to spawn. Unlike the salmon, steelhead don't die after they spawn. They can return to the ocean and grow larger. Some think this makes the steelhead fight harder than a salmon. Others say steelhead are more intelligent than salmon and the people who fish for them. Steinbeck said, "It has always been my private conviction that any man who puts his intelligence up against a fish has it coming."

Research has indicated the intelligence of fish matches or exceeds that of the higher vertebrates, including non-human primates. This should come as no surprise. The first fish on Earth date back before the age of the dinosaurs. The first modern humans appeared a mere 40,000 years ago. Fishing has gotten a whole lot tougher since then. In the evolutionary scheme of things, if the history of the fish could be represented by the width of the Olympic Peninsula, the history of humans would be a speed bump somewhere west of Oil City.

Fish possess a cunning, manipulative social intelligence that allows them to learn by watching the experiences of others. Fish are intelligent enough to join that exclusive club of creatures we call tool-users by using rocks to free themselves from lures. Fish use gravel to build nests on the stream bed after navigating many thousands of miles across a trackless ocean to return to the place where they were born. Some fishermen even have a theory or an excuse that steelhead have become so highly evolved they can untie knots under water with no hands. If this is true it could explain why fishing is bad and getting worse.

Fishing for winter steelhead has been described as a mental condition with no known cure. There is only a palliative therapy that can be as bad as the disease. Just getting to the river can be a real accomplishment. The hazardous winter driving conditions can be the steelhead's greatest natural defense. Highway 101 can be a treacherous frozen snake of a road in winter. You'll want to keep an eye on the log trucks. If the logs are wet, it means it's raining ahead. If the logs are white, it means snow. Sometimes the road is closed by landslides, snow-slides and fallen trees tangled up in the power lines. This is perfect. It keeps the tourists from ruining the fishing. You can have a chance to float the rivers without getting rammed by another boat. Sometimes the State Patrol will advise against driving on Highway 101 unless it is absolutely necessary which would define steelhead fishing for many of us. We're fishing for the largest steelhead that swim the earth. It is a quest for the dinosaur of trout, a fish that survived the Industrial Revolution. It is a fish that should not exist but it still does. Fishing for the dinosaur steelhead is a form of time travel back to the good old days. Sometimes when the light is right and the fog is thick on the river you can feel as if you are the last person on earth. You can forget what time or day or year it is because in the depths of the rainforest winter none of those petty distinctions matter. It can be a hundred years ago; the same fish are still swimming this river.

The winter steelhead fisherman is a strange critter. Many have evolved an extra layer of fur and blubber as an adaptation to the extremely wet and cold conditions. This enables them to fish in weather that's far too violent to go to work in. Once the line freezes into solid chunks in the rod guides fishing becomes even tougher. That's when you're liable to see some poor soul trying to suck the ice out of his rod guides so he can make one more cast.

Steelhead fishing can require layers of rubber, wool and fleece for survival. Chances are by the time you put on enough clothes to stay warm while steelhead fishing, you won't be able to move. That's okay; you may have what it takes to be a plunker. These are people who sit and wait for the fish to come to them. All you need is a large fire, patience and more patience. Others prefer casting their gear out into the river and bouncing it downstream until it snags on something. Then you have to break off your line and tie on something else. Typically, this will happen about every second or third cast. Fishing for steelhead can be very expensive, especially if you have no idea how to catch one.

Many people try to spend their way into a first steelhead by buying the most expensive gear they can get. This seldom works. Buying steelhead tackle is a road to financial ruin made worse by the certain knowledge that you are just going to throw it all in the river anyway. This only enhances the quest for the legendary secret lure. I need another secret lure like I need a hole in the head. Don't get me wrong; secret lures can be the secret to good fishing. The trouble is the effectiveness of a secret lure can be brief. It depends upon fish runs, the height of the water and the number of people using the secret lure that can make it not a secret anymore. Typically, about the time you find a secret lure, it will stop catching fish and you have to find another one. It can be a very frustrating to shop for a secret lure. That's because in any display of fishing lures in a tackle store, there are the empty spaces that indicate certain lures have sold out. Those were the lures that caught fish, the ones that aren't there. You can go ahead and ask if they'll sell you the lures that aren't there, but chances are all you'll get is attitude.

The best way to get a secret lure is to find one on the water where it was fished. One day I noticed a funny colored plug floating down the middle of a smooth stretch of river. Then I saw a large boil and a silver flash of a steelhead just underneath the plug! If a fish would bite at a plug floating on the surface, I wondered if it would work on the bottom of the river. It did. That plug caught fish until the paint was eaten off it. It kept catching fish, even after it was chewed down to bare plastic. It didn't matter what color the plug was. It must have been the action or the shape of it the fish liked. Sometimes the secret of a secret lure remains unknown. I mourned the day that plug was lost. The secret lures you find generally share several identifying features, such as bent hooks, scratched paint and maybe some broken line still tied on. These are clues the lure was badly abused. It's the one you're looking for. Plugs and bobbers can be found where they washed into back eddies with the flotsam. Sinking lures are generally on the bottom of the river, which can make them tougher to get. The rewards can be great. A root-wad stuck in a good fishing hole can snag enough lures to start a tackle store. Retrieving this treasure trove is not without its hazards. Just ask the guy who hooked the winch on the front of his pickup to the small end of a gear-grabbing snag in the Hoh River. Things went OK at first. Then the big end of the snag caught the current and started dragging the truck sideways, toward the setting sun.

The best way to find a new secret lure is get it out of the mouth of a fish that you caught. You may have to catch many hundreds of steelhead to find a secret lure with this method, but nobody said it was easy. None of this matters to someone who wants to catch a fish. In fact, if you start accounting for all the time, money and effort that steelhead fishing demands, it may be time to hang it up and get a life.

Once you find your secret lure, it's time to learn how to cast it. I have always been very proud of my trick casting ability. I don't think it's bragging to say I was once able to cast a lure high into the air and have it land in my shirt pocket. That is a talent that takes years of practice. I think it is way past time to have trick casting included as an Olympic sport. While casting may not have the glamour and excitement of gymnastics or beach volleyball, trick casting requires a special skill to hit a small target with a lure at a long distance. There are strict rules with winners determined by the number of lures lost. Unfortunately, the results are largely self-reported. It's easy to tell if a trick caster is lying about how many lures they have lost: his lips are moving. Real trick casters don't have to lie, but they just might out of a force of habit.

The fish have spent their entire lives watching people throw secret lures at them. By the time a fish has reached adulthood, they have pretty much seen every fancy cast there is, except one. As a fishing guide who fishes over 500 days a year I was able to develop a cast the fish have almost never seen before.

It is called the "Suicide Cast" because if you fail to execute properly, you will lose everything on the tree limb. Done properly, the "Suicide Cast" will not only amaze and delight any witnesses who happen to be present it will cause the fish to attack like hungry sharks.

Though difficult to master, this presentation simulates a mutant tree creature falling in the river creating a feeding frenzy.

Rookies often make the mistake of trying to retrieve the lure from the tree limb. I have found it is much better to strip out line and lower the lure into the river. This allows you to fish water that would have been way out of range if you hadn't cast into a tree. Slowly I let out line, lowering the lure from the tree limb until it just touches the surface of the water. Chances are the fish have never seen a cast like this before.

The "Desperation Cast" is a high-arching backhand over-the-shoulder maneuver that should only be used after you have given up hope of ever catching anything. Be sure to give yourself plenty of room before using this cast to avoid hooking anxious onlookers who are trying to copy your technique.

If the "Desperation Cast" doesn't work, you may need the "Kamikaze Hurricane Cast" to score. This is a sideways presentation that almost tips the boat over and hurls the lure with the low angle trajectory of a rifle shot through tree limbs and between logs with amazing results.

A word of caution before using this particular cast: The more physical force you put into the "Kamikaze Hurricane Cast," the greater the likelihood something will go wrong. If you snag yourself or others while attempting the "Kamikaze Hurricane," it will guarantee a trip to the emergency room. You could be through fishing. That's when you might have to make the trickiest cast there is, "The Last Cast." The great thing about "The Last Cast" is you can always make another one. I've seen guys stand around for hours making "The Last Cast." With any luck at all, no cast is really your last.

People who don't fish and there are some, claim steelheaders are insane but compared to what? A steelheader who has just spent the day on the verge of hypothermia is thrilled with the prospect of a nice warm rain. It will make the rivers rise and bring in more fish. What if we have another nasty cold snap on the way? That's great news to a steelheader. It will make the rivers drop back down into perfect shape. All weather is good weather for the delusional steelheader.

Some fishermen even claim they have heated drift boats to deal with cold weather. A drift boat heater is a propane powered torture device that is useful in hair removal. Drift boat heaters have led to documented cases of spontaneous human combustion. A drift boat heater can come in handy, melting your line when you least suspect it. The truth is an open boat is all but impossible to heat. Anyone who claims to have a heated drift boat is either a liar, a guide or both. Boat heaters can be tricky. Usually about the time you feel your feet starting to thaw out in front of the heater your boots are on fire. At precisely that moment a silver torpedo of a fish jumps out of the river. People start screaming at you. You try to reel in the fish with icy fingers in frozen mittens that accidently push the free spool button on the reel. This causes a huge bird's nest of tangled line that breaks with a crack like a pistol shot as the fish heads back downriver. You sit in a cloud of smoke from your burning rubber boots and can't wait to do it again.

You ask yourself the eternal question: why did I lose that fish? Even if the fish did not actually untie the knot steelhead have many other ways to get lost. They swim at the angler at a high rate of speed. The humans become confused when their line goes slack. While the steelhead use the slack line to swim around and break the line on the many rocks and sticks in the river or the hook just falls out because our angler is too busy sulking to reel in the line.

If the fish is still on, they have another trick that is almost sure to work. They shoot to the surface and start shaking their head straight at the poor confused human who thought he had lost the fish. That's when all those years of watching bass fishing shows finally pays off and he jerks that rod straight up in the air just like they do on TV. Once you get a steelhead to the surface of the water, you are not liable to lift them any higher. The steelhead know this so they just shake their head until the hook pops loose leaving our angler to collapse in despair realizing they may have lost the fish of a lifetime.

It doesn't really matter how big a fish of a lifetime is. Some people fish for steelhead all their lives and never catch one over 15 pounds. Others claim to have caught 40-pounders.

Either way catching the fish of a lifetime can lead to depression and a feeling of inadequacy that can directly translate into other areas of your personal life. At first just watching the fish of a lifetime peel out 100 yards of line and jump into the sunrise can allow you to forget your dead-end career, abusive relationship and nagging health problems long enough to enjoy life. The sordid details are pushed to the back burner when you hear the words "Fish on!" These two words have been known to release endorphins into the bloodstream that can adjust serotonin levels in the brain in a manner consistent with other forms of addictive behavior.

The symptoms of a fish-induced psychosis can take many forms. Typically, the beginning angler starts out happy to catch one steelhead a day. They think that is good fishing. As the season progresses however, they are driven to catch another and another fish to get the same buzz they used to get catching just one. They may go on fishing binges that can last for days, the only purpose of which is to catch larger and brighter fish. The mystical connection between man and fish is reduced to a delusional statistic of numbers caught on the days spent fishing. The angler may wear rubber boots when it is not raining. They obsess on the weather report. They may smell like fish. They develop physical maladies like minor burns on their thumbs caused by hot fish peeling line off the reel. Or they may suffer from tennis elbow without ever having played the game. They got it from setting the hook on one too many fish. They may develop problems at work, that is, if they still have a job. Few employers enjoy having production stopped just so the crew can look at my fish pictures or listen to the one-that-got-away fables that only foster an inbred sense of failure.

At that point, there is nothing you can do but wait until the angler hits bottom. The day will come when they can't catch a fish if it's flopping around in the bottom of their boat. This will often cause the poor angler to pause and reflect on the pointless nature of their existence. They find themselves wishing they could just catch one really big fish.

Many lives have been ruined by big fish. There is the sullen realization that no matter how hard you search, you will never see another fish like that in your lifetime. As the memories and the stories of the one that didn't get away are embellished through the years, the trophy will tend to grow larger long after it is freezer-burnt. The fish you catch for the rest of your life will seem smaller and less significant. You will be driven to a vain attempt to catch another fish as big as the big one but this will probably fail since we are only allowed one fish of a lifetime.

All of this can leave you with a sense that there is nothing left to live for. You are just going through the motions of fishing without any real sense of self-validation, enjoyment or revenge. You feel spawned-out, slack-bellied and headed downstream tail first in the river of life. You find out your so-called fishing friends are jealous back-stabbers now that you caught the fish of a lifetime. They go around saying you either snagged that fish of a lifetime at the hatchery pond or bought it from the tribal gill net fleet. They say you really should get that fish of a lifetime mounted. That's easy for them to say. They don't have to explain the cash for the taxidermist to the significant other who informs you they will Feng Shui that stuffed fish out in the garage the minute you bring it home. Later you'll be forced to hock the stuffed fish to the divorce attorney, which would explain why there are so many trophy fish on the walls at law offices. The best thing to do if you catch the fish of a lifetime is to make sure there are no witnesses, turn it loose and don't tell anyone.

The best example of a fish of a lifetime ruining a life occurred a few years ago, when anglers from far and wide were shocked and awed by the tragic death of a wild steelhead on the Hoh River. It was a monster steelhead thought to be about 30 pounds. The fish's killer was a fly fisherman with no prior fishing incidents or known motives. He claimed to have been innocently casting his Spey rod for 10 years in the Hoh River without a bite when tragedy struck. The unlucky angler claimed the fish was hooked by accident. A struggle ensued. While the results of an autopsy were not available, witnesses claimed the fish was bleeding from the gills after dragging the unlucky fly fisherman around the river for an estimated 45 minutes.

Once the fish was on the beach, the real trouble started. The fish-killer described the tragic death of the fish in every newspaper in the Pacific Northwest saying the trauma, stress and emotional scarring of killing the fish put a knot in his stomach. He had no idea that putting a piece of sharp steel into the mouth of a creature might actually harm them. The steelhead killing was witnessed by a number of nosy fishing guides who immediately blabbed to the internet. This set off an inquisition of cyber-bullies who were too busy on their computers to go fishing themselves but seemed to know more about it than everyone else put together.

It was with great reluctance and the statute of limitations that I was able to confess the real reason the killer fly fisherman was able to land his fish of a lifetime: The fish was tired. My boat had already caught and released the fish earlier that day. I wanted to get a picture of the giant steelhead, but the batteries in my camera were dead and besides, the client said he was in the Federal Witness Protection Program and did not wish to be identified for the safety of his family and loved ones. It's all about family to me. I was very proud of releasing that fish back into the river to swim upstream. That is, until it was killed by the fly fisherman.

The only thing worse than catching the fish of a lifetime, is to not catch one. It happens. Some days we don't catch anything. Poor fishing can help us appreciate the days we caught fish and teach us new excuses for failure. Fishing excuses allow for the wide range of changing conditions. The Hoh River is famous for getting as much as 200 inches of rain a year. This abundant rainfall not only grows some of the world's largest trees but also provides abundant year-round excuses for not catching fish. Once it stops raining, you'll have to come up with another fishing excuse.

I'll never forget the morning there was a mysterious bright light shining through the fog.

The light appeared to be moving slowly upward and getting brighter until you could hardly look at it. Disturbed, I was about to dial 911 but I couldn't remember the number. I tried to remain calm so my fancy friends in the front of my boat wouldn't panic.

"That sun sure feels good," one of them said, trying to put up a brave front.

"Oh yes, the sun," I said like it hadn't been raining for so long I forgot what the sun looked like. It was pretty. It was a good time to have a nice cup of frozen coffee. I tried to chip the coffee out of the cup with a knife I'd been using to clean the fish. This made for a-fish flavored espresso that could indicate just how bad you can need that morning coffee.

The sunshine reflected across the smooth green surface of the water to the white-barked alder forest that lined the shore. After a while the temperature soared to over 40 degrees Fahrenheit, which is just too darned hot for me to fish in. Some people claim they like sunshine and blue skies, but that's not what we call steelhead weather. If you have to fish in the sun, it's better to fish with the sun shining up the river, the same way the fish are facing. That way the fish have the sun at their backs and they can see the lures coming downstream flashing in the sunlight. The sun is one of the greatest fishing excuses ever made. Sunshine warms glacier and turns the river gray. The fish won't bite. Not only that, the sun can get in your eyes. Having the sun in your eyes is one of the greatest excuses for fishing or any other activity.

Blaming sunshine opens the door to a whole new world of fishing excuses where but for a simple planetary alignment you would not be such a failure. Remember it's not your fault if you can't catch a fish, it's too sunny. Unfortunately, the "weather is too nice for fishing" excuses only work until the weather changes. This is where a whole new kit of excuses must be employed. Let's say you are on a river that is swarming with salmon but you cannot catch one. There could be many reasons for this, such as the stage of the moon, atmospheric pressure or the temperature of the water is all wrong. Feel free to use any of these excuses. I have used them all at one time or another and they seem to work. The only fishing excuse that doesn't work is: I didn't go.

42

PEARL HARBOR DAY.

"December 7, 1941 – a date which will live in infamy." President Franklin D. Roosevelt said these words many years ago. Today, Dec. 7 might mean one less shopping day until Christmas, but it means something else to "The Greatest Generation," the people who fought World War II.

The debate over whether Roosevelt knew of the impending attack on the Pacific Fleet bottled up in Pearl Harbor continues to this day. Whether the attack on Pearl Harbor was indeed a surprise or a cynical manipulation in a geopolitical chess game didn't matter to my mom at the time.

Mom's cousin Jack Abernathy, U.S. Navy, got bombed at Pearl Harbor. That got her Irish up! It was payback time for Tojo. There was a war on! Mom could see the need for long-range strategic bombers in America's war against the Axis Powers. She found a sleepy little airplane factory down along the Duwamish River in her home town, Seattle. In no time mom had the Boeing plant whipped into apple pie order. At one point in the war she was rolling a B-17 Flying Fortress out the door every 49 minutes! Powered by four 1,200 horsepower engines, the B-17 could carry a crew of 10 at speeds of up to 250 miles per hour. It could cruise 400 miles with a ceiling of 35,000 feet. Most importantly, the Flying Fortress could fly even when it was "shot to hell."

Cousin Donny (Donald Abernathy, Army Air Corps) always said

he worked at a flower shop in the war, no. He was a tail gunner in a B-17, flying support for Uncle Jack's (Jack Lopresti, U.S. Army) European Expeditionary Force. The B-17 specialized in precision daylight raids, which made them an easy target for the Germans' deadly accurate 88mm Flak guns.

After the Battle of Midway on June 4, 1942, the United States began an island campaign to protect America's lifeline to Australia. At midnight Aug. 6, 1942, the U.S. Navy's first amphibious assault began on Guadalcanal. To protect the landing mom's B-17s turned the Japanese fleet headquarters at Rabaul into what Admiral "Bull" Halsey called "rubble" while bombing and strafing Japanese reinforcements attempting to retake Guadalcanal.

On Nov. 1, 1943, my uncle Len (Leonard Neal, U.S.M.C.) landed in heavy surf on Bougainville with the 3rd Marine Corps to face an estimated 35,000 tough, veteran Japanese troops of the 6th Imperial Division infamous for the Rape of Nanking. Meanwhile a Japanese naval force of two heavy cruisers, two light cruisers and six destroyers was approaching to shell the beachhead where the Marines were dug into shallow foxholes in the pouring rain.

Fortunately, Navy Task Force 39 of four light cruisers and eight destroyers ambushed the Japanese using torpedoes and radar to range their guns in a night action that forced a sudden retreat and saved the beachhead that was only 50 miles away.

Uncle Len and about 34,000 other troops established a defensive perimeter one mile deep and five miles long while the Seabees finished the impossible task of turning swamp into an airfield.

Meanwhile Mom was determined to march north and secure an airbase that was within bombing range of Tokyo. The rugged 30-mile long island of Guam was ideally suited for the Japanese defenders when a combined force of U.S. Army and Marine veterans of Guadalcanal came ashore on July 21, 1944. Over 3,500 Japanese and 1,500 Americans died in a battle that continued in isolated pockets until the end of the war. The last Japanese soldier on Guam did not surrender until 1972. My Dad (Duane Neal, U.S.N.) ran an airfield on Guam for Mom's long- and medium-range bomber fleet to conduct reconnaissance and bombing missions.

Once Uncle Len's Marines had secured Bougainville, he headed north to help General Douglas MacArthur return to the Philippines where an estimated quarter of a million Japanese troops were waiting under the command of General Yamashita, the "Tiger of Malaya." On Oct. 21, 1944, an estimated ton of explosives was fired ashore for every man going to the beachhead with MacArthur at Leyte. Once again Uncle Len's invasion force was saved from annihilation by Japanese battleships by Dad's Navy in what has come to be known as the greatest naval battle in history: the three-day Battle of Leyte Gulf that all but wiped out the Japanese Imperial Fleet. Meanwhile the Leyte invasion was stalled in a campaign reminiscent of the Western Front of World War I and forced the postponement of MacArthur's optimistic invasion schedule for a month.

As Dad and Uncle Len's island-hopping offensive drew closer to the Japanese home islands, both sides refined their tactics into more horrifying desperate measures. Admiral Onitsha sent bomb-laden fighter planes to crash into American ships. Named after the Divine Wind that scattered the Mongol fleet of 1281, the Kamikaze became one of the most effective weapons the Japanese used as a defense against the U.S Navy.

In Feb. 19, 1945, the U.S. Marines landed on Iwo Jima to secure an airfield so Mom's planes had someplace to land if they were shot up trying to bomb Japan. The Japanese defended Iwo Jima with a series of caves and dugouts that withstood the pre-invasion bombardment and waited to ambush the Americans when they could inflict the greatest casualties. The B-17 was the Marine's best friend on Iwo Jima, precision bombing enemy positions right next to the front lines.

By 1945, Mom was building the larger B-29 bomber. On March 10, 1945, 350 of her B-29s dropped 2,000 tons of magnesium, phosphorous and napalm on Tokyo, incinerating 16 square miles and killing 100,000 people. It remains the single deadliest attack ever inflicted on a civilization. Despite these heavy casualties, the Japanese military continued a fanatical but hopeless defense. That was until mom's B-29 Bombers dropped two atomic bombs on Japan.

Mom built that bomber fleet, riveting them together in eight-foot sections, one plane at a time until the war was over and there was peace. After the war, Mom went on to create the post-war boom in America. She never let on that she was a war hero. Just another patriotic American teenager doing her part to bomb the Axis Powers back to the hell they came from. Thanks, Mom, from a proud son and a grateful nation.

43

THE CHRISTMAS LETTER

This is a special time of year when the warmth and joy of the holiday season can drive you right over the brink. Each day is one less shopping day until Christmas. It wouldn't be so bad if there were just 12 days of Christmas. Somewhere things went horribly wrong. Now Christmas kicks off after Labor Day. By the time December rolls around, it seems like Christmas really does last all year if that's how long it takes to pay for it. Maybe it's because we've been sucked into a road-to-nowhere marketing strategy that sells the "best Christmas ever" ideal. If this year is the best Christmas ever, logically it would mean last year's Christmas sucked and next year's will be a dud. Meanwhile chances are we'll endure just another mediocre Christmas where our mailboxes clog up with Christmas catalogues, Christmas cards and that other holiday flotsam, the Christmas letter.

With few variations on the basic theme, the Christmas letter usually consists of from one to several pages of fantasy about the perfect lives of deluded freaks who must live on another planet somewhere and it's a lot better than the one we're stuck on. You know the ones: They always brag how lucky they are and how good they got it. They got a job. Grandma got out of rehab. They made out like congressmen from an insurance settlement they got by wrecking their truck. Others use the Christmas letter as an excuse to rub our noses in their medical problems or even worse, try to sell you stuff. Some of the worst Christmas letters even plagiarize lines from literary classics in an effort to sound intelligent. I'm not bitter, but anything they can write, I can write better.

It was the best of years and the worst of years for me. My most triumphant highlight had to be the Oil City Skunk Cabbage Festival and the Skunk Cabbage Festival float, a massive 40-foot tall skunk cabbage floating above a carpet of brown algae. That float represented many thousands of hours of labor by the Oil City volunteer staff. It kept them off the streets and gave meaning to their simple lives. That's what the Skunk Cabbage Festival means to me, helping others.

After the Skunk Cabbage Festival, the Hoh River Lavender Festival proved the old adage: build a better bug trap and the world will beat down your door. I made so much money selling lavender bug traps at the lavender festival I hurt my back sitting on my wallet. Each of my Guide Model Lavender Bug Traps comes with a genetically engineered fish head inside a sleek plastic bucket. Be sure to get your bug trap today with the enclosed order form so you'll have one in time to protect your loved ones from the insect plague this coming bug season.

This past year was an excellent year for bugs. My years of research finally paid off when I landed a big endorsement deal from an insecticide company that sells bug-proof underwear. Every outdoors person owes it to themselves to get a set. I have enclosed an order form with this year's Christmas letter for your convenience. Maybe the bug-proof underwear would have come in handy when I got abducted by aliens last summer while on a camping trip. Those little buggers play rough. I woke up the next morning with a sun burn and a headache. There was a big circular burn mark from the mother ship right in front of my tent. The next thing I know some forest rangers showed up and accused me of having an illegal campfire. It's a sad day when an honest fisherman has to take the rap for some pesky aliens that can't read a sign that says, "No Campfires". I don't need that kind of hassle with my medical condition. I just came through another Christmas colonoscopy. Check the enclosed order form and I'll send you a video of my colonoscopy just in time for the holidays with your choice of a complimentary set of bug-proof underwear or a casual yet elegant guide model bug trap. Whatever you wish to order here's wishing that you and yours have the best Christmas ever!

THE CHRISTMAS COLONOSCOPY.

It was daylight on the river but I was not on the river. This was strange since I was on a fishing trip of sorts. It was a fishing expedition up my colon. The holidays are full of the spirit of the season when we celebrate the joy of giving with sugar plums, fruit cake and the Christmas colonoscopy. The holiday season can be an extremely stressful time of year. You can't say "Merry Christmas" without fear of offending someone. The fact remains that no matter how many different religious, pagan and corporate ways there are to celebrate the holidays, we all share a common colon. It's something we can all celebrate together.

There are some people who are just hard to shop for. Like your abusive boss or your underhanded, overbearing coworkers. You know the ones. Santa put a video game in their stocking last Christmas Eve, and by Christmas morning the ingrates said it wasn't violent enough. We all have someone in our lives we'd like to open a picture of our colon on Christmas morning. We owe it to ourselves to let that special someone know just how we feel. A colonoscopy is diagnostic, therapeutic and the perfect springboard for my new reality TV career. My agent said it was a part that would get me more exposure and expand my career into limitless horizons.

The network was going to call it "Colonoscopy with the Stars." Each week, celebrities would drop by for a picture of their colon. A panel of judges, audience members and all the folks at home would match the mystery colon to the celebrity guest for cash and prizes. The celebrity lineup for the initial CWS episodes included some of the biggest colons in show business.

Sensing competition, I knew I had to get my own colonoscopy before the other show business weasels stole my idea. I checked into the plush celebrity colonoscopy suites that had been specially reserved at the medical center. The TV was excellent. I could just imagine seeing myself up there on the small screen giving the greatest performance of my career.

But first I had to answer a series of skill-testing questions, like what was my name and was anyone threatening me with physical violence. I told the nurse that of course I was being threatened. As a wilderness gossip columnist, the list of individuals, organizations and government agencies that were not threatening me would be a lot shorter. Then I got very sleepy. I went to a happy place with champagne wishes and Viagra dreams where I had sent everyone in the world a picture of my Christmas colon.

When I awoke, my adoring fans said I gave a perfect performance. There were tears in the judges' eyes. That's what it's all about. To provide a shining beacon to the little people too numerous to mention who made my reality TV career what it is today. If I had but one Christmas wish, I would borrow a phrase from a favorite Christmas carol: May your days be merry and bright and may all your colonoscopies be right!

45

THE PERFECT TREE.

The best way to eliminate holiday stress is to shelve outdated notions of the perfect-Christmas syndrome. This is not a perfect world. Do you think the first Christmas was perfect? Jesus was born in a barn! Christmas doesn't have to be perfect, unless you're talking about the perfect Christmas tree. I've always been very proud of cutting the perfect Christmas tree. We're not after just any tree here. We are after the perfect alpine fir Christmas tree.

"Abies Radiocarpal" grows high in the Olympic Mountains and there's snow up there in December. Any Christmas tree expedition had better be prepared for blizzard conditions on treacherous roads. It's a good idea to carry enough survival gear to stay alive until rescue. Sometimes you have to hunt around for a while to find a perfect Christmas tree. That's because the tree's degree of perfection occurs at an inverse ratio to its distance from a road. They say you should always tell someone where you're going on a Christmas tree hunt and when you are coming back. Except the locations of the perfect tree patches are a closely guarded secret I won't give away.

A low winter's sun found me at the end of the road where the climb up the side of the mountain began. There was only a foot of snow, but it had a good crust that made it perfect to skid a tree back down the hill. I considered taking a tarp along so the tree wouldn't lose any needles, but then I thought I'd pack light when I took a look at the hill. I started climbing. By the time I remembered I'd forgotten my water bottle I was sweating like a walrus. At least I remembered the axe. It was sunset when I reached the crest of the ridge. I'll never forget the view. It looked like a burning city of clouds the night before the end of the world. There was nothing to do but keep going. I needed a perfect tree and the holiday stress was mounting.

Then I came out into a clearing in the forest and there was the perfect tree. It was perfectly symmetrical without a limb out of place. There were little cones in the branches near the crown. I shook the blanket of snow loose and noticed the strangest thing. There was a bird's nest in the lower branches. It looked like the nest of a Canada jay. This tree was so perfect it was already decorated for Christmas with strands of silver lichen strung through the branches. I remembered the old Indian curse about messing with a Canada jay nest but it was getting late. This was a perfect Christmas tree. I cut the tree down.

It was starting to get dark. The belly of a moon showed through the clouds so I could see pretty good until I got in the timber. That's when I lost the perfect tree. We started sliding down an icy slope. It was me or the tree so I let go. After a while I worked my way to the bottom of the cliff the tree fell off. The top was busted, but I figured I could haywire it back together with a big star and nobody would know. I took off my belt and used it to lower the tree down the mountain. This was tough to do with my pants falling off.

I knew I was getting closer to the road once I hit an old clear-cut. As I dragged the tree through the overgrown logging slash, the cones, bird's nest and a lot of the bark and needles were stripped off the tree. A couple of limbs were broken clear off. None of that mattered once the tree tumbled down onto the road where my truck was parked. I'd found the perfect tree.

46

CHRISTMAS ON A BUDGET.

It's no secret that the holidays cause a lot of holiday stress. I suppose anything worth doing is worth overdoing. These days it's every American's duty to spend money like a drunken sailor at Christmas to maintain the standard of living that makes our country so cool, unless you can't.

Then all it takes is a little imagination, a few gallons of gasoline, a strong stomach, some rubber gloves and a respirator to turn Christmas on a budget into an adventure the whole family can enjoy.

The Olympic Peninsula is not only a recreational wonderland filled with hiking, biking and nature activities galore. The back roads of this emerald jewel paradise have become a not-to-be-missed dumping ground for many of the local inhabitants. To judge from the refuse, recreational dumping is a family affair where you load up the truck with toys, furniture and animal carcasses and head for the freedom of the hills to dump it all up in God's country.

Call it dumping with a view. Some of the more picturesque dumps allow the dumper the thrill of rolling major appliances, engine blocks and offal off a cliff to watch in child-like wonder as it bounces down the mountain. Other more accessible dumps spread the inventory in a wider area allowing the scavenging Christmas gift bargain-hunters more choices for their Christmas list.

Often the people who dump garbage are multi-taskers, dropping off unwanted pets with their refuse. While I have long supported a spay-neuter program for pet dumpers, until that happens you have a good chance of picking up a cute little puppy or a box of adorable kittens at your next visit to a wilderness dump. Who wouldn't want to share that with the joy of the holiday season?

Have an automotive enthusiast on your Christmas list? You're in luck. Many hard to find parts for rare subcompacts lie strewn about the forest floor. Sometimes entire vehicles with as yet undiagnosed mechanical difficulties and minor burn marks lie just under the road awaiting a little TLC to get them purring again.

Sure, you may have to sift through a ton of garbage, dirty needles and waste oil containers to get a real Christmas treasure like an exercise bike. That just makes each gift more special. Call it giving something back to nature or leaving a piece of themselves, the forest dumpers have left private dumps throughout the woods for the rest of us to discover and enjoy.

These "boutique" or "designer dumps" are found in places like the Dungeness watershed, where just downstream thousands of people get their water. I once asked a forest ranger why they didn't do like they do in more civilized countries like Montana or Idaho: put a dumpster at the bottom of the logging roads to avoid polluting the aquifer.

"That would never work because people would just fill the dumpsters with garbage," the forest ranger said. Of course, why didn't I think of that? And besides, dumpster-diving could take a lot of fun out of the Christmas recycling experience. Part of the attraction is the thrill of the hunt.

Here's hoping you find the Christmas dump of your dreams!

THE SOLSTICE

Looking upriver that December day
    I had to squint in such a way
    To look into the Solstice light
    That turned the water silver white
    And looking downriver from where I came
    Lay an abysmal canyon the light disdained
    Astride the border where light and dark meet
    I could see only what lay at my feet
    Blind to the future forgetting the past
    I could but hope this peace would last.

48

CHRISTMAS GIFT IDEAS.

We've often heard the question asked, "Why can't Christmas last all year?" Are you insane? Just think of the staggering costs in terms of the human suffering brought on by holiday stress and the endless decisions you are forced to make. Will this Christmas be cash or credit? Will this Christmas be at home or on the road with seasonally adjusted holiday fuel prices and a crumbling transportation infrastructure that makes you want to kiss the ground when you finally make it to your destination? Meanwhile, the money we spend on the holiday season determines the health of our nation's economy. Here are a few more last-minute must-have items you can stick in an angler's sock that are guaranteed to produce squeals of joy on Christmas morning.

3-D Magnifying Glass: You'll need these to read between the lines of our ever-increasing fishing laws. Don't leave home without them.

Heated Pole Holder: This can be a real hassle but worth the extra expense for quality time on the splash deck.

Guide Model Fish Scale: Did you ever wonder why some fishermen just seem to catch bigger fish? It's simple really; you just have to have the right gear. My new Guide Model Fish Scale will have you boating 20-pounders trip after trip while the rest of the ham-and-eggers are lucky to catch one 20-pounder in 10 lifetimes. Using a patented secret method, the Guide Model Fish Scale adds up to 40% more weight on any fish you catch.

Guide Model Measuring Tape: It's the law. You may not remove the rare and endangered bull trout from the water while releasing it. You still want to know how big it is. By simply measuring the length and girth of the fish with this device, it's possible to calculate almost any weight you want. Fisherman's 3D Magnifying Glasses not included.

Fisherman's Lie Detector: More than just a surefire way to get to the bottom of a murky fish story, the Fisherman's Lie Detector has all the makings of a party game the whole family can enjoy. Just attach the sturdy Velcro cuffs and headband, then turn up the voltage and flip the switch to see just how big the big one that got away really was. The Fisherman's Lie Detector is not recommended for those with heart conditions or dentures.

Tackle Box on Wheels: Impress your fellow anglers and organize your gear with a tackle box as big as all outdoors. It's a known fact that fish are just tougher to catch these days. So, if you plan on catching one of today's super-intelligent fish, you will probably need a secret lure to do it. As any angler will tell you, one secret lure is never enough. The Tackle Box on Wheels, with its sturdy wheelbarrow suspension will not only carry a lifetime supply of secret lures down to the river, it may even help you walk upright. The mule needed to drag Tackle Box on Wheels is not included.

49

CHRISTMAS SURVIVAL GUIDE.

Christmas can be very dangerous starting with 'Black Friday.' This opening of the Christmas shopping season can be a bargain-hunting riot where people have been beaten, pepper-sprayed and trampled to death trying to get consumer electronics at up to 60% off.

Got your shopping done? It's time to put up the Christmas lights! According to the Consumer Product Safety Commission, in 2010, more than 13,000 people included a visit the emergency room as a part of their Christmas celebration to treat broken bones, cuts and burns that they got from decorating. Up to 16 decorating deaths and 100 house fires from circuits and wiring have been reported in one year.

Let's put up the tree. The Christmas tree is more than just a symbol of pagan tree-worship used to celebrate the birth of Jesus; it has been described by fire officials as a "bomb in the middle of your house," which, according to the U.S. Fire Administration, causes an average of 11,000 house fires that injure 250 people with 40 fatalities every year.

Let's open some presents! On average, more than 2 million dangerous toys and children's products are seized by the CPSC every year before they can reach the hands of children. Still in one year, more than 250,000 people were treated in emergency rooms due to toy-related accidents.

An average of 6,000 people a year go to the emergency room

as the result of a psychotic condition known as "wrap rage" where people injure themselves trying to open hard plastic packages. The last time I tried to open a package of batteries it was like field dressing a deer except the blood was my own!

Then we throw the package away with the rest of the 5 million tons of Christmas garbage (including wrapping paper, ribbon, tinsel, greeting cards, broken toys, etc.) while producing 885,000 tons of carbon dioxide, 4,800 tons of sulfur dioxide, and 2,800 tons of nitrogen oxide to make the extra electricity to light up all of those houses, shop windows and Christmas trees.

Christmas is also a time when the pressures of money and an increase in alcohol consumption place additional strains on relationships. Ask any law enforcement officer and their worst calls are for domestic violence, which seems to increase during the holidays.

Still got sugar plums dancing in your head? Sugar and refined carbohydrates are linked to diabetes. Researchers around the world have come to the conclusion that the consumption of refined sugar is detrimental to the health of people without diabetes and disastrous for those with it. Then it is time to carve the turkey! Americans consume over 22 million turkeys on Christmas Day! Although turkey contains a natural sedative called tryptophan, the chemical doesn't have a large effect because it's mixed with everything else you eat. That "food coma" you experience is the result of your body working overtime to digest all that food. A study conducted by the National Institutes of Health found that the average person's weight gain during the holidays is just over 1 pound. Sounds harmless, but the researchers found that the extra holiday weight was still present a year later on 85% of study participants. Gaining one extra pound each year can add up significantly. Christmas can be hazardous to your health but it is survivable. Shop local, buy American and thank God Christmas doesn't last all year.

50

THE BEST CHRISTMAS PRESENT.

Christmas is about giving and receiving gifts. I think the best presents you can get are the ones that give joy to others. I can think of no better example of Christmas joy than the year I found a duck call in my Christmas sock. Blowing a duck call around the Christmas tree is one of my most cherished Christmas memories. It created a holiday ambience that allowed grandma to relax and take out her hearing aid. The duck call seemed to infect the rest of the family with a contagious Christmas spirit. Mom suggested I go outside and walk around the neighborhood with my duck call just like the carolers did. I went from one house to the other quacking up a storm but nobody seemed to be home which seemed a little strange on Christmas morning.

After I had been practicing with my duck call for a few hours the phone rang. A hunting buddy had also got a new duck call for Christmas. His family insisted he join me for a Christmas duck hunt, somewhere. That was a lucky break. It was his turn to be the retriever. Watching a well-trained retriever work is one of the greatest thrills of duck hunting. I often wished I had one but mom said we could only have one dog and my sister picked it out. It was a basset hound.

At the time, I had no way of knowing that basset hounds detest water and won't retrieve anything they haven't eaten first. I spent years trying to teach that dog to swim, often up to my waist in freezing water. Only to find out the poor creature was allergic to feathers. We were not about to stop duck hunting just because the bird dog went on strike. We figured it was a simple matter of doing it yourself if you wanted it done right.

My duck-hunting buddy and I took turns being the retriever. There was no sense in both of us drowning for the same duck. We thought we would get in big trouble for that especially on Christmas. We looked on the bright side. The water in the Strait of Juan de Fuca is actually much warmer than the atmosphere in the dead of winter. We were duck hunters. Nobody said we were smart.

I'll never forget the Christmas I thought I lost my retriever. We had shot a duck in the surf. It was my friends' turn to swim. The duck was floating away, so my retriever lost no time in launching into the surf with a cedar slab for flotation. The duck was playing possum. Just as my retriever was about to make a grab, the duck took off swimming for Vancouver Island. I offered to shoot the duck again, but the retriever started whining about getting sprayed with birdshot. Toughen up. My retriever took off after that duck until they were both well out of range. I never went hunting with quitters.

After a while my retriever looked no bigger than a kelp head. I figured a rip tide got him. It was lonely on the beach after that. But my retriever had left me half a box of shells. There was pie and Christmas cookies in his lunch box. Later that day my retriever washed ashore with a big saw-billed fish duck. I was so glad to see him I didn't care if he wanted to beat me up for eating his lunch and shooting all his shells at more ducks that he had to retrieve. It was his turn.

51

THE GIFT OF THE GUIDES- WITH APOLOGIES TO O. HENRY.

Eighteen dollars and fifty cents, that was all. Most of it was in quarters and dimes saved one at a time by bargain hunting the tackle stores for hooks, fishing line and the other essentials for life on the river. Bella and her husband, Ray Bob, lived on a plunking bar along the lower Hoh River. Plunking was a lifestyle choice where you built a fire, tossed some fishing gear into the river and waited for migrating steelhead to pick up your lure as they swam by. Bella and Ray Bob had moved to the river to go fishing, but it was snowing too hard to fish.

Ray Bob was a fishing guide and nobody was going to pay to go fishing in a blizzard so bad you couldn't make it to the boat launch. Bella looked out onto the gray river under a gray sky and knew that they'd be broke for Christmas. Bella counted the money three times, had a good cry, and then powdered her cheeks with some egg cure Ray Bob had left on the kitchen table.

They had met while fishing on the river. Ray Bob had given Bella a fly he tied himself. He tied one on. She cast the Dungeness Special as smooth as maple syrup, clear across the river without a ripple on the water and snagged a big spawned out bull trout right in the pectoral fin. The enraged bull trout tore up river like an enraged beast. It bent Bella's fine bamboo rod nearly double, and stripped the drag washers off her reel. If there was one possession in which Bella took pride, it was her fine bamboo fly rod made from Tonkin cane her daddy brought back from the war. It was such a fine rod that if Bella and the Queen of Sheba ever fished on the same river, Bella would out fish her 10 to 1 using dull hooks.

And if King Solomon himself ever showed his face on the river with all his fancy fishing tackle, he'd be humbled by Ray Bob. He fished the Ray bobber. Ray Bob had been named after the Ray bobber. It was the best steelhead lure ever invented. No longer manufactured, the Ray bobber could only be found out on the river, after it had been lost by another fisherman. Ray Bob had the largest collection of Ray bobbers in the country. The trouble was he had no place to put them. What Ray Bob really needed was a tackle box for his Ray bobbers. Until now, Ray Bob had kept all his lures in a five-gallon bucket. It was humiliating watching him empty his lures out on the beach every time he wanted to tie one on.

Eighteen dollars and fifty cents, it was all the money Bella had for Ray Bob's Christmas present. She took her fine bamboo rod down to a tackle store. There was a sign in the window that said "We buy fishing gear." She sold her fine bamboo rod at the tackle store and bought Ray Bob a gift, a tackle box for his ray bobbers. With the money left over, she got a tuna pole with a roller tip.

By 7 o'clock, the hot buttered eggnog was ready. Ray Bob came through the door of the little travel trailer. There were holes in his rain gear. He had leaky hip boots. His eyes settled on the tuna pole.

"What happened to your fly rod?" he asked.

"I sold it to buy you a present. Here, it's a tackle box on wheels. It's big enough to hold all your Ray bobbers," Bella said. "It might even help you walk upright."

"That's a nice present," Ray Bob said, "but I sold all of my Ray bobbers so I could buy your present. Here, it's a brand-new fly reel."

People give gifts at Christmas to commemorate the Magi giving gifts to the Christ child. The Magi were wise men. Nobody ever said fishing guides were wise. But they still give the best gifts they have.

52

ANOTHER CHRISTMAS CAROL – WITH APOLOGIES TO CHARLES DICKENS.

Humbug! I huffed and I puffed my way through the lobby of my newspaper tower, The Oil City Blotter, crammed as it was with holiday well-wishers yammering their loathsome clichés of merry this and happy that.

"Merry Christmas!" a soon-to-be-former employee gushed, staring at me as if demanding something – a raise, a parking spot or a day off. My hand went for the pepper spray kept for just such occasions.

"Merry Christmas?" I gasped. "Christmas is about good news. We sell bad news in the newspaper business. If it bleeds it leads. We'll have no Merry Christmas here."

I ducked into the newsroom, an airless warren illuminated by a single lump of burning coal where the staff gathered around to thaw their fingers. There they kept very well.

"Humbug!" I said. "Do you think coal grows on trees? I might as well cancel the Christmas party now that you've burned your Christmas present!"

"Please Mr. Scribe sir," the staff begged, "We've been scrimping and saving all year to buy your Christmas present."

"That must mean I pay you too much. Make a note."

"Yes Mr. Scribe sir."

Seething, I made my way to my executive suite at the top of the tower. I was late for a deadline on a story about the true meaning of Christmas. It seemed as if people just used Christmas to take advantage of my generous nature, after all I'd done for them. It was out of the kindness of my own heart that I supplied the coal, the rain barrel for drinking and washing and the daily gruel in the lunchroom, and all they could come up with was one crummy little present for me at Christmas.

Maybe they think running a newspaper empire that at one time stretched from Shine Slough to Whiskey Flats is easy but it's not. It took me years to become an overnight excess. Then everyone wanted a piece of the pie. Like the gaggle of do-gooders that was clogging the hallway to my office. They were collecting money of course, for of all things, "The Old Guide's Home," yammering about pity for the less fortunate.

"Pity for the less fortunate? Why waste pity on anyone but yourself?" I demanded. "This is Oil City. Can't they be realtors? Is the casino closed?" That set the beggars packing off to bleaker pastures. I was left to discover the true joy of the Christmas season. At 6 in the evening I gave the staff the rest of the day off. It was after all, Christmas Eve, the culmination of months of marketing, fundraising and muck raking. There was nothing left for me to do but go home to my walled compound and find the true Christmas Spirit.

What is Christmas anyway? There has to be more to it than buying things you don't need, with money you don't have, for people you don't like, who won't remember. Or you can give guilt, the gift that keeps on giving. Either way, it's only a small part of a disturbing big picture. I saw a vision of Christmas past. The poor staff was toiling in a frozen newsroom while I went fishing.

Then I saw a vision of Christmas present, the workers freezing in the dark while they scrimped and saved for my present. It was then I realized that in the past year I had done a lot of things to forgive myself for. That is the Spirit of Christmas. Forgiveness is a revolution in the evolution of human thought. Jesus forgave his killers saying they knew not what they did. If Jesus forgave us, can we forgive others? If we forgive others, can we forgive ourselves?

That was a big order. I'd just written a year's worth of horrible stories. At first, I wanted to share my love of nature. That went over like a skunk in a punch bowl. Then I bad-mouthed the government. Give up on that and we'd have very little to talk about around here. Then I wrote about holidays and their awesome toll of human suffering, but it was okay, I mean compared to the rest of the stuff I wrote. I was able to forgive myself.

Then I woke up. It was Christmas morning. I'd found the true meaning of Christmas. I beat it down to the newspaper. No one was there. It was a good thing I'd given the staff the day off. There was a punk in the alley on a skateboard.

"Do you know about the 100-pound salmon the old poacher snagged out of the hatchery pond?" I asked.

"Sure do, that fish is as big as me," the boy said. "It's still hanging in the smokehouse."

"Then here's $100, lad, if you can get that fish and fetch it back here in an hour."

"Yes sir!" the punk wheeled away. I never saw him again. Merry Christmas and God bless us everyone.

53

CHRISTMAS ON THE HOMESTEAD.

Sometimes when feeling overwhelmed by the stress of the modern holiday season I think of a story that was told to me by an old pioneer about Christmas on an Olympic Mountain homestead during the early years of the last century.

"Our farm was an old homestead claim. Pa had to go pretty far up the river and into the mountains to find land and when he finally did it was covered with trees which were considered worthless. There was no way to grow anything until he cut the trees down so he could plant something between the stumps. Once he had a crop there was no way to sell it to anybody because the neighbors were growing the same things that they were trying to sell to him and the city was just too far away to pack the crops to town. Pa dug a root cellar into the side of the mountain to keep the potatoes, cabbages, onions and carrots from freezing through the winter. I think winters were harder back then. One year it started snowing at about Thanksgiving and did not let up until sometime after the new year. We called it the winter of the blue snow because it piled up so deep.

That was the winter the bobcats ate all our chickens so we had no eggs. Spring had been wet and cold. The bees didn't wake up in time to pollinate our fruit trees so we had no apples. That summer a bad hail storm knocked down the oats and ruined them so we ran out of feed for the cow and we had no milk. The cabbages were eaten by a new kind of worm that no one had ever seen before. The potatoes got some kind of black mold that made a lot of them rot in the ground before you could dig them. What onions we grew were small and pitiful. The only thing that grew very well that summer was rutabagas. They are a kind of hybrid between a turnip and a cabbage that us kids didn't like very much. Ma tried to mix the rutabagas with potatoes and onions which wasn't too bad but then we ran out of potatoes and onions. Not even the animals seemed to like rutabagas. We fed them to the chickens before the bobcats ate them and the eggs tasted like fish. We fed rutabagas to the cow and the milk tasted sour while it lasted. It was a good thing Pa shot a deer so we had some fresh meat for a while. The rest of it was salted and dried into jerky by hanging it in the rafters of the cabin. As it got closer to Christmas us kids were all excited. Pa was taking the hides of the chicken-eating bobcats to sell in town. You never knew what he'd come home with. One Christmas it was peppermint candy. One year we each got an orange.

By Christmas Eve we could only imagine what wonders this year would bring. Ma shaved the jerky into a pan of hot water to make a gravy that would go with the rutabagas. She scraped together enough flour to make a Christmas Cake and sent us out into the woods gathering dried bark for the cook-stove. It was lucky I took the shotgun along because I got a grouse for Christmas dinner. Pa came home just at dark with some wonderful news. He'd shot a wolf on the way to town and collected the bounty. We all got new shoes. It was a Christmas I'll never forget."

54

THE DAY AFTER CHRISTMAS.

How was your Christmas? Mine was the best ever. Say what you want about peace on Earth and good will towards men but for the rest of us, Christmas is all about the presents. Remember the bad old days how we were brainwashed into thinking that the size of our Christmas haul was determined by whether we were naughty or nice? Forget that. I was a bad person all year long and still got a big pile of the coolest presents from Santa anyway. The day after Christmas I took all that stuff back to the store where it came from and got what I really wanted in the first place: video games.

I doubt there is a better way to share the warmth, joy and magic of the Christmas season than by playing video games. Especially when you're playing the biggest game series in the world, Call of Duty. The latest version Black Ops 2, takes you from dense jungles to exploding cities where you run through a computer-generated world shooting people with your choice of weapons that can either "kill or subdue!"

After a few hours of shooting people on the screen, I got a cramp in my trigger finger. It was time for a nice relaxing drive. That's where Grand Theft Auto comes in. GTA is a 3D, digital feast where you find yourself in a world of gangs, crime and corruption. Things do not go well. I don't want to ruin it for you, but GTA players soon find themselves exploring a world of urban mayhem where they rob the liquor store(s), steal cars, run over pedestrians and elude the police. The great thing about GTA is that the game gives you an empowered sense of freedom where you can throw grenades and Molotov cocktails, in other words, do pretty much whatever you want. In the soon to be released GTA 5 (in HD!), one character even pours gasoline around a truck and lights it on fire! How's that for holiday fun! Grand Theft Auto is the kind of Christmas gift the whole family can enjoy but there are many more that can help make this holiday your best ever.

Mortal Kombat is a free-roaming action-adventure game that uses martial arts to destroy your opponent with a finishing move called a fatality. This allows the victor to either murder their defeated, defenseless opponents in a gruesome manner or engage in a suicide race to see if the winning player can finish off the losing player before the loser can kill themselves first.

Hitman is a stealth action adventure game. That means you can choose from a whole big bag of dirty tricks to kill people instead of just using raw firepower to blow them away. Here you play a cloned assassin for hire. Your weapons include fireplace poker, pool cues and a special fiber wire that allows you to bypass metal detectors so you can garrote your enemy when they least expect it. Your goal is to kill assigned targets and no one else. You may kill any witnesses but any unnecessary murders count against your final score, unless you kill them by accident. As a hit-man you may sedate, poison, blow up and burn your target, or even disguise yourself as a doctor and sabotage a surgical procedure. The possibilities are endless! In most cases, you are required to hide the body unless you leave it out in the open for all to see.

No matter how you play them video games are the kind of Christmas present that makes the perfect gift for the whole family to enjoy.

NEW YEAR'S RESOLUTIONS.

By now we've all had it up to here with know-it-all-drive-by-lap-dog-cookie-cutter-newspaper columnists preaching imaginary New Year's resolutions they have no intention of keeping themselves. The most important thing to remember about New Year's resolutions is to avoid unrealistic expectations like world peace or catching a 40-pound steelhead. The lower your expectations, the more likely you'll keep your New Year's resolutions. Focus on the little things you can do to make your life better and allow you to reach your full potential.

New Year's Resolutions usually include getting organized, learning new things and helping others. Last year I said I was going to get organized starting with my tackle box collection. Hoarders always say we are going to get organized, someday. That's instead of throwing the junk away! There are many reasons for this. It's probably because if we actually went to the dump we'd find another tackle box that just needs a little duct tape and a bungee cord to be a proud addition to a growing tackle box collection.

Then there's my collection of broken fishing rods. The worst part of being a fishing guide is watching someone break a fine custom rod. Unless you're watching yourself break your own fine custom rod. I thought if I saved enough broken rods I could match an unbroken tip section to an unbroken rod butt to make one good rod. After collecting a 50-gallon drum of broken rods, I came upon the cruel realization that it's always the tip section of the rod that breaks, leaving you the butt section that is too short to fish. Getting organized is just another pointless exercise in futility.

I was going to learn some new things last year, but who was I kidding? What made me think I could ever speak Canadian, eh? I had to watch an entire hockey season to figure out what a hat-trick was. Learning new things is pointless since the more you learn, the more there is to know. The human brain is only capable of processing so much information at a time. Learning new things can make you feel stupid. Take it from me: ignorance really is bliss.

Then I decided to help others by translating the fishing laws into English. Talk about your unrealistic expectations. Helping others is often futile. Some people won't let you help them help themselves and others are beyond help. Helping others can make you feel used. In reality, these pathetic New Year's resolutions are nothing more than empty promises and sad admissions that last year was a failure and the coming year is liable to be just as bad or worse.

There is however, a New Year's resolutions we should all try and keep. It's fun, cheap and so easy you can do it with your eyes closed. You can do it alone or with another person. You can probably get away with doing it at work as long as the boss doesn't find out. It's good for you and we all need a lot more of it and that is sleep.

Last year my New Year's Resolution was to get more sleep but there was no time. In spite of all the time-saving gizmos in our modern world of the future, there is an acute shortage of time. The demands on our time are time-consuming. We as a society have spent years killing time despite the fact we can't make any more of it. Sometimes it seems like there's no time to do nothing.

Archaeological studies have shown that doing nothing is a distinctive human trait that separates us from the animal kingdom. In prehistoric times, early man did nothing to increase their use of leisure time, which was a prerequisite for the development of civilization. The whole point of civilization was to allow some people to do nothing.

Scientists are only now discovering the health benefits of doing nothing. Studies have shown you can do nothing to lower your heart rate, respiration and blood pressure. Doing nothing indoors is a good way to avoid exposure to the sun's harmful rays. Doing nothing may be the best course of action we have to combat climate change. Sleeping and doing nothing can decrease the size of your carbon footprint. This does not require energy, which makes these affordable, sustainable, environmentally responsible activities the whole family can enjoy. Even better, our politicians haven't dreamed up a permit or tax for sleeping and doing nothing yet, but don't give them any ideas. Given the sluggish state of our economy, you probably think you don't have enough money to do nothing, but take it from me, you're never too broke to do nothing.

That's why this year for my New Year's resolutions, in addition to getting more sleep, I'm going to do nothing. Join the millions of others who are already doing nothing. There's nothing like it.

56

NATIONAL READER(S) APPRECIATION DAY.

Thank you for reading this. Sometimes I think that if you didn't read this column no one would. But you do. I can tell from all of the wonderful cards and letters that you send. To show my appreciation for this tremendous outpouring of emotion it might be a good time to review the reader(s) letters policy. Please remember that even the simplest thoughts from the most confused brains can be more effective with proper spelling. For example, "Kill" is spelled with two "l's". "U" is actually spelled "Y-O-U." Maybe you should use a little more glue on those letters you cut out of your bass fishing magazines when you try to glue them together into words on the butcher paper. Words can be hard to read when the cut-out letters spelling the words are all jumbled up together in the bottom of the envelope.

While each letter writer should feel free to celebrate their diversity through the free and open expression of crazy ideas without danger of facing the ridicule of others, these suggestions are meant as constructive criticism for clearer communication. I am only trying to help by suggesting you work on your scissors skills. That's if they still let you have sharp objects. Still, even if they don't let you have scissors anymore and you're nothing but a glue-sniffing bass fisherman, that does not make your opinion less valuable.

National Reader(s) Appreciation Day is a time to thank the

reader(s) who put on their galoshes to wade out through the snow in the pre-dawn darkness of a Monday morning to fetch the newspaper only to find to their consternation that the column is not there. Then call me later to complain until I explain, the column has always been published on Wednesdays. That's when I realize that every day can be National Reader(s) Appreciation Day. Thank you for reading this.

Printed in the United States
By Bookmasters